The Seasons of Hope

The Ray S. Anderson Collection

Ray Sherman Anderson (1925–2009) worked the soil and tended the animals of a South Dakota farm, planted and pastored a church in Southern California, and completed a PhD degree in theology with Thomas F. Torrance in New College Edinburgh. He began his professional teaching career at Westmont College, and then taught and served in various administrative capacities at Fuller Theological Seminary for thirty-three years (retiring as Professor Emeritus of Theology and Ministry). While teaching at Fuller, he served as a parish pastor, always insisting that theology and ministry go hand-in-hand.

The pastoral theologian who began his teaching career in middle age penned twenty-seven books. Like Karl Barth, Prof. Anderson articulated a theology of and for the church based on God's own ministry of revelation and reconciliation in the world. As professor and pastor, he modeled an incarnational, evangelical passion for the healing of humanity by Jesus Christ, who is *both* God's self-revelation to us *and* the reconciliation of our broken humanity to the triune God. His gift of relating suffering and alienated humans to Christ existing as community (Dietrich Bonhoeffer) is a recurrent motif throughout his life, ministry, and works.

The Ray S. Anderson Collection comprises books by Ray Anderson, an introductory text to his theology by Christian D. Kettler, two edited volumes that celebrate his distinguished academic career (*Incarnational Ministry: The Presence of Christ in Church, Society, and Family* and *On Being Christian . . . and Human*), and a reprint of an Edification volume that focuses on Ray Anderson's contributions to the field of Christian Psychology. A word of gratitude is due to The Society of Christian Psychology and its parent organization, The American Association for Christian Counselors, for their permission to make the *Edification* issue available in book form. Jim Tedrick of Wipf and Stock Publishers deserves a special word of thanks for publishing many of Ray Anderson's books and commissioning this collection of works to continue his legacy.

Todd H. Speidell, General Editor

The Seasons of Hope

Empowering Faith Through the Practice of Hope

Ray S. Anderson

WIPF & STOCK · Eugene, Oregon

THE SEASONS OF HOPE
Empowering Faith Through the Practice of Hope

ISBN 13: 978-1-55635-814-2

www.wipfandstock.com

Manufactured in the U.S.A.

Contents

Preface

"For everything there is a season, and time
for every matter under heaven."
(Ecc. 3:1)

There is something to be said for letting the rhythm of life carry some of the risk. In the world of nature, both plants and animals have their seasons of fertility, of mating, of shedding the old, and of beginning anew. When we become strangers to the earth we have lost more than our roots; we have lost touch with the rhythm of life. Where once there was rhythm there is now repetition and routine. Where life once was seasonal and secure it is now episodic and erratic. We live 'after the fall' as playwright Arthur Miller once wrote, 'unblessed' on earth and unconnected to heaven.

If we have the means we can compensate for this loss. We can keep our houses and cars at an even temperature, no matter how hot or cold outside. We can, if we wish, buy fresh fruit in the winter and go ice-skating in the summer. We can go to the zoo to see animals in their 'natural habitat', wear synthetic fiber that feels like 'real wool,' and furnish our homes with 'authentic' replicas of traditional furniture.

It does not work of course. We knew it all along. In the depths of our soul the blessing we seek remains illusive. The life and work that is unblessed is impoverished and futile. We can make the movements but lack the rhythm. We dance when there is no music and weep when there is no pain. We seek for what novelist Thomas Wolfe once called, "the lost lane-end into heaven."

Perhaps this is not true for all of us, but every life has its moments when the music stops and we are left stranded without a partner. When what is lost cannot be recovered and what lies ahead cannot be seen, our hopelessness feeds on helplessness. But it is just at this point (in time!) that the broken edge can become the growing edge. We need to rediscover and reenter the rhythm of life; this is what I know.

My father used to plant potatoes every spring. First we would cut them into pieces, making sure that each piece had an 'eye' in it, as he called it.

From this 'eye' a sprout would form and then the pieces were ready to
be placed in the ground. One thing remained however before we could
plant. To ensure a good harvest of potatoes, my father said that we must
plant them when the moon is full. So we would wait until the propitious
time, and then place them in the ground.

The calamities that can befall a potato crop are no greater than other
misfortunes to which farmers are subject. The fact is, potatoes are among
the least vulnerable vegetables to disaster given sufficient water and an
occasional spraying for potato bugs. And we only planted a few rows
for our own table use! So why this annual nod toward the cosmic 'potato
god'? I can only explain it as a relic of folk-lore and, if I dare say so, a small
and harmless way of placing the whole of his life within the rhythm of
nature. The moon also has its phases and if one is going to march to the
beat of nature's drum, it does not hurt to get in step!

We always had sufficient potatoes come fall as I recall. In those days
I did not venture to submit this folk wisdom to a scientific test by deliberately planting some during another phase of the moon. I doubt that he
did either. It was probably the only superstition that I recall my father
ever including in his otherwise common sense approach to the tilling of
the soil and the husbandry of our livestock.

Even as I write this, why do I feel a sense of uneasiness in making such
a clear distinction between superstition and common sense? He would not
have been happy with such a charge. For him the working of the soil was
a participation in a cycle of sowing and reaping, suffering crop failures
and rejoicing at bountiful harvests. He never disclosed his inner feelings,
neither of grief at his losses nor joy at his successes. I gather now that he
lived a self-life in communion with the seasons of nature with the rhythm
of birth, life and death and, yes, by the phases of the moon! This may be
the most common of all senses.

This I know. My father kept his inner life in step with the seasons. He
connected much of the risks of life as well as the pain to the rhythm of
life. The planting of potatoes in the full moon was a kind of sacrament, a
communion with nature. It was his way of getting in step with the rhythm
of life, permitting that rhythm to carry some of the risk.

Planting potatoes in the full moon is after all, only a metaphor which
points toward the uncertain relation between what we do with our lives
and what comes of our lives. This is the risk, that the factors that we cannot control, the events that we cannot predict, and the evil that we cannot
prevent will cause everything we do to fall to ruin.

That which consecrates the tasks we undertake is not success, but that we who do these tasks are participants in the longer and larger pilgrimage of life. My father was not just a farmer who raised crops but he was a husband, brother, father, and godparent to the children of others. He regularly attended the funeral services held for others in the community who died and carried the caskets of many to the grave. In no way could a crop failure due to uncontrollable or unpredictable forces rob him of his value and place in the community. He let the rhythm of the community with all of the seasons of human life bear him along, taking the risk for him.

Life itself contains a rhythm when we see it from beginning to end. Our personal existence is not a series of individual episodes taking place as 'points in time.' Rather, life itself bears us along in a common pilgrimage. At any given time we are part of a community where birth and death, joy and sorrow, pain and pleasure, as well as sowing and harvest are taking place. This communal sharing of life replicates all the 'seasons of life.' For every time in our life there is a season in the life of the human family. This rhythm of human life is meant to carry the risk of each person's existence.

There is a rhythm of blessing and celebration of each individual life. The blessing of the newborn baby for instance, is not only a religious ritual having its antecedent in the blessing of the children by Jesus (Mark 10), but it is the human family's way of bearing the risk of that child's life. This child belongs, this child counts, this child's life is woven into the 'quilt' of the community in such a way that there will always be a place for it no matter how irregular its shape!

There is a rhythm of Sabbath rest that is given to creation as a divine covenant. Without the Sabbath, which literally means the seventh day, the curse that binds human life to toil and futility would be fatal. Within the story of creation itself there is placed the Sabbath interlude. "Thus the heavens and the earth were finished, and all their multitude. And on the seventh day God finished the work that he had done, and he rested on the seventh day from all the work that he had done. So God blessed the seventh day and hallowed it, because on it God rested from all the work that he had done in creation" (Gen 2:1-3).

The repetitive phrase, "from all the work that he had done," reminds us that work is to be followed by rest. The point of work is not found in the work alone, but in the finishing of it. There is a rhythm in creation. There is work and then the work is finished, and then there is rest.

What is the lodestar that guides us through the seasons? What draws us forward from one time to another when the burden of the past grows heavier while the lure of the future grows dimmer? Some say that it is nature itself. As the bear awakens in the spring after hibernation, and the squirrel stores up nuts for the winter, humans also move at the impulse of blind instincts. That would be so easy if it were true. Words like 'faith,' 'dreams,' 'failure,' 'hope' and 'despair,' would not then be in our vocabulary. Yet they are, and one cannot erase the words without destroying something that makes us more than animals. "But we had hoped," confessed the two disciples after the death of Jesus (Luke 24:21). Caught in the depths of despair, their dreams of following the Messiah into a glorious Kingdom shattered by a crucifixion, they were blinded to the reality of his presence. When hope dies the spirit fails, and the seasons lose their power to rejuvenate the spirit. 'Keep hope alive' is more than a slogan coined to raise the spirits of the oppressed and marginalized in society. Hope is the lodestar ahead of us and the light burning within us. It is hope that keeps faith on course.

Faith is the sail that we raise in hopes of catching a friendly breeze bringing us at last to the safe harbor of our desires and dreams. Without hope faith is susceptible to the fickle winds of fortune and fate. The author of the book of Hebrews has in mind a slightly different metaphor but captures the same truth: "We have this hope, a sure and steadfast anchor of the soul, a hope that enters the inner shrine behind the curtain, where Jesus, a forerunner on our behalf, has entered, having become a high priest forever according to the order of Melchizedek" (Heb 6:19-20).

The inspiration for our faith is poured into our hearts from the wellspring of hope. The Apostle Paul assures us that "hope does not disappoint us, because God's love has been poured into our hearts through the Holy Spirit that has been given to us" (Rom 5:5).

There is a kind of hope that does disappoint us. False hope is a siren song enticing faith to raise its sails when there is no wind, as many have learned to their sorrow. On many an occasion, when facing the loss of what we value the most, we 'keep our hopes up' that some miraculous intervention will occur and grant us our heart's desire. When our hope is finally crushed by the unavoidable reality of life, the sails of our faith lie tattered and torn at our feet. In one of the Peanuts strips created by the late Charles Schultz, Lucy stood in the outfield with a fly ball approaching. "I hope I catch it," she said, pounding her glove. "What happened?" cried out Charlie Brown, when the ball dropped untouched in front of her. "Hope got in my eyes," she replied.

In this book I will argue that hope is a spiritual virtue, and as such it has its 'times and seasons.' "Hope that is seen is not hope," the apostle

Paul reminds us. "But if we hope for what we do not see, we wait for it with patience" (Rom 8:24-25).

In my youth I was more fascinated and taken up with harvest time than planting time. The drudgery of chores in the winter and the bleak days of early spring planting seldom stirred my soul. The care of the crops during the hot days of summer was a battle against weeds, insects and the worrisome weather. I had no positive feelings for these days and duties. My emotions were fixed on harvest time! My father, however, had learned through some failures to harvest a crop, to invest his hope in the spring planting rather than the fall harvest.

Life is best lived from one sowing to another, not one harvest to another. The good harvest is a time of rejoicing and thanksgiving at life's bounty. But those who live by the harvest, die by the harvest. If harvest is all that stirs the heart, what is left when the harvest fails?

Life is a venture where good fortune is desired and misfortune is feared. When we venture our life in relationships and undertake commitments where it is possible to lose what we love the most, we can experience a loss for which there is no insurance or means for compensation. A loss of that which we have loved and in which we have made investments of passion and patience, is heartbreaking. It can lead to an empty and broken life.

From this I learned that hope for a harvest without the planting of the seeds is a precarious way to live. Sowing is quite different than reaping. When we sow the seed in the soil we are exercising hope by investing our time, energy and sometimes our limited resources, in the power and promise of life. Sowing is an investment of something precious to us in utter dependence upon the promise of a harvest through a power over which we have no control. This is as good a definition of hope as I know.

When we envision the planting of new seeds, we have looked past the ruins of a failed harvest with hope toward the coming spring, a time of growth and renewal. Preparing for a harvest takes only a few days, or even hours. Preparing to sow new seeds requires months of waiting through the long winter, anticipating the warm spring sun and the stirring of the soil. Sowing has to do with preparing the seed, preparing the soil, and attending the new growth. All of this is the exercising of faith empowered by hope.

The metaphors of nature, the seasons and vineyards run like a stream throughout the Old Testament. Israel is portrayed as God's vineyard (Isa 5:30). Jeremiah says of his people, "They have sown wheat and have reaped thorns" (Jer 12:23); and he laments, "The harvest is past, the summer is ended, and we are not saved" (Jer 8:20). One third of Jesus' parables (10 of 31) have to do with seeds, sowing, harvesting and with growing things. The apostle Paul speaks of common wisdom when he says, "Whoever plows should plow in hope and whoever threshes should thresh in hope of a share in the crop" (1 Cor 9:10. "You reap whatever you sow," he warned, using a natural metaphor to capture a spiritual truth (Gal 6:7), and speaking of hope, he adds, "for we will reap at harvest time if we do not give up" (6:9).

These metaphors not only remind us of how closely we are attached to nature but also of spiritual realities of a supernatural form that impinge upon our daily lives. My own life on the farm, both as a young boy and later operating my own farm, brought my soul under the discipline of the seasons. For this reason, this book is experiential though not biographical. Hope is at the core of everyday life. And everyday life is a reality check of our spiritual life.

I had thought of writing about faith, but decided that hope is more seasonal than faith. One might have hope without faith, but faith would be impossible without hope. Faith, in the biblical sense, is a gift (John 1:12-13), while hope is the fruit of endurance and character (Rom 5:3-5). As a quality of character, hope is 'home grown.' Our inner life is like a garden where we cultivate the seed of hope and experience the power of hope to receive and live with the gift of faith.

Using the metaphor of the four seasons, I want you to explore with me the ways that we can sow the seeds of hope, cultivate and nourish hope, reap the harvest of hope, and then repair and renew our hope as a continuous cycle of spiritual empowerment and growth. Each of us is at some point in this cycle. Or, we may have lost our rhythm and are living and working 'out of season.' With hope, there is always a place to begin, and to begin again.

Part One

SPRING

The Generation of Hope

Nathan
February 10, 1992

There are rolling hills toward which I glance
where prairie winds move the grass to dance
in celebration of sacred vows,
the rooted rhythm of a chlorophyll chorus line,
quite oblivious to the roving advance
of the grazing cows.

I choose the leeward side of the sloping hill
and lay where the close cropped grass still
smells sweetly of bovine breath;
I staunch the bleeding of the severed grass
with my cheek, and promise never to kill
what lies this side of death.

A spirit from the depths of God's eternity,
stirs the stillness of what is yet to be,
a birth to bless this temporal place;
I feel the touch of an infant's breath
brush 'cross my cheek, and rise to see
myself in his boyish face.

Thrice removed by each generation
our lives are linked by each separation,
we meet in those we love;
For you, my son, I've claimed heaven's promise
and embraced on earth the joyful consummation
of God's gift from above.

The wind visits the same green hills, if by chance
the cows still graze and the grass will dance,
but the boy has left his lonely station;
when you see his face in your own reflection
you will recognize in his knowing glance
that you are NATHAN!

                                                        RSA

<u>Chapter 1 - Preparing</u>

Separating the Seeds from the Needs

Seed is precious. For one who lives by the power of the seed, most everything else is consumable and disposable. As demanding as the appetite sharpened by incessant hunger may be, the seed for next season's sowing cannot be made into daily bread. During the drought of the 1930s, when the harvest was meager, the first things that were saved were the sacks of wheat for sowing next spring. I remember them, stacked safely in the small shed, still exuding the faint fragrance of the summer heat, untouched while the animals survived on weeds cut and dried from the edges of the barren fields. No questions were asked and no answers given. The seed spoke for itself. Its destiny was sealed by hope and thus beyond our immediate need, more precious than the few silver coins that could only be spent, and with them, the spender's hope as well.

In her poignant sonnet, Edna St. Vincent Millay, captures both the anguish and the hope in a loss that must be grieved, and survived.

> The broken dike, the levee washed away,
> The good fields flooded and the cattle drowned,
> Estranged and treacherous all the faithful ground,
> And nothing left but bloating disarray
> Of tree and home uprooted. . . was this the day
> Man dropped upon his shadow without a sound
> And died, having laboured well and having found
> His burden heavier than a quilt of clay?
> No, no, I saw him when the sun had set
> In water, leaning on his single oar
> Above his garden faintly glimmering yet. . .
> There bulked the plough, here washed the updrifted weeds
> And scull across his roof and make for shore,
> With twisted face and pocket full of seeds.

She could as well have written, a pocket full of hope, for in that small hand-full of seed there is hope that can multiply itself beyond our comprehension.

The seed is a miracle. It is a miracle of multiplication. The exponential power of a single seed is staggering to the imagination. A single ear of corn of average length (8 to 10 inches) can produce up to 400 kernels, each of which, if planted produce at least one other ear, yielding 160,000 kernels, each of which, producing 400 more could yield a total of 64,000,000 in just two generations. In just a few years, the total amount of corn produced from one kernel could cover the entire face of the earth several feet deep. I will leave it to my grandson who has a high SAT score in math, to determine how many years and how deep!

How long can a single seed survive with the power to germinate and grow? The oldest seed known to germinate and produce a living plant was discovered during archaeological excavations at King Herod's palace on Mount Masada near the Dead Sea. Its age has been confirmed by carbon dating as over 2,000 years. Planted on January 25th, 2005 in a nursery on the kibbutz in Israel's Arava desert, the date palm has five leaves and stands 14 inches high and is nicknamed Methuselah after the 900 year-old biblical character. A seed lying dormant since the birth of Jesus still carries within it the miracle of life and hope. Surely there is a parable here. Lying perhaps unnoticed or long forgotten in the soil of every life there is a seed of hope that only requires some attention and care (prayer!) in order to grow like a "root out of dry ground" (Isa 53:2). But you have to find the seed in order to discover the power of hope.

But not every seed is meant to carry the burden of hope. Some seeds betray us by their early appearance only to fail to deliver the harvest for which we hope. "He was just sowing his wild oats," my father once commented, when a young man in our community neglected his farm and family by indulging in some frivolous activities that got him into some minor problems with the law. Indeed, there is such a plant as wild oats. Like a weed, the plant grows in the same field as the oat seeds that were sown. It resembles oats, but when mature its own seed was virtually nothing but chaff with no substance. In every harvest of oats there were always some of these 'wild oat' seeds along with other seeds, that could be discerned by an expert eye. Woe to the farmer who carelessly sows weeds among the seeds! This is why preparation involves separation.

Sifting Weeds from the Seeds

In times past, a farmer dipped his hand into a sack of seeds saved from a previous season and scattered them on prepared soil in hopes of producing a future harvest. All in all, it worked quite well. A bushel of seed can yield a wagon-load of grain, weather and insects permitting--a miracle so commonplace that one can perform it without invoking divine assistance. As to the weather and insects, however, the gods are not infrequently consulted—or blamed!

The miracle worked equally well with every kind of seed. One wonders how many eons passed before the discovery was made that some of the weeds that mysteriously appeared amidst the growing grain, competing for nutrients and moisture, were sown along with the seed. What was gathered in the harvest of one year was being sown promiscuously in the year following. Nature works according to its own laws. You reap what you sow—it makes sense. All science begins with common sense. The raising of grain became a science when seed selection made more sense than sowing everything that was in one's hand.

One of my tasks as a small boy on the farm was turning the small 'fanning mill' as it was called, while my father poured the wheat seed in at the top. The apparatus consisted of a series of screens or sieves of different sizes so arranged that what was poured in at the top passed over these screens as they were shaken from side to side, with the wheat seed flowing in one direction while the smaller weed seeds went in another. The crank that I turned by hand caused the sieves to shake and the fan to operate, blowing away the dirt and chaff. The weed seeds were fed to the pigs and the clean wheat seed planted.

Yet, all was not well. The wheat that grew from these seeds often developed diseases that stunted its growth and reduced the yield. It was suspected that something in the soil was hostile to the emergence of the plant from the seed. Only by the time that I began to farm for myself was it known that the micro-organisms that caused the problem could be identified and destroyed. Not only did I make sure to plant seed that was free of weeds, but the seed was chemically treated before it was planted in order to resist the diseases which lay waiting in the soil.

Essentially what we were doing in sowing and reaping was little different from that which was practiced by the first humans on earth—the laws of nature had not changed. Every sowing is a generation of hope, as it has always been. "In the morning sow your seed, and at evening do not let your hands be idle; for you do not know which will prosper, this or that, or whether both alike will be good" (Ecclesiastes 11:6).

Not Every Need Should Become a Seed

"I think that I know what a need is," a member of my adult class at church said. "When I gratify a need it usually leads to some disappointment or even worse, a real loss of personal self-worth. But how can I tell the difference between a need and a seed?" I responded, "You are asking the wrong question. What you need to ask yourself is, What eventually do I want to be or what kind of life do I want to have?"

I have a friend who is a financial advisor. He told me that when a client asks about planning for the future, the first thing he asks is, "What kind of retirement do you envision? How much income will you need to live a life-style that you want? What kind of needs do you anticipate for long-term health care?" These are the questions, he told me, that determine what kind of investments, savings or other commitments need to be made in the present in order to achieve the long-term benefits. This is exactly how to determine what a 'seed' of hope is. One does not just look at seeds, one looks at what kind of 'harvest' is desired and then selects the seed that will produce that outcome.

For example, good character is a fruit; it is produced through a thousand moments in which one chooses to keep a promise, to fulfill an obligation, or to make a contribution to others rather than settle for mere self-gratification. It is, in a sense, to be a 'righteous' person, not just a religious person but a person of integrity. "The Lord watches over the way of the righteous, but the way of the wicked shall perish" (Ps 1:6). It should also be noted that this is a 'nature Psalm,' the righteous are planted where there is living water and their fruit prospers (1:3). In another Psalm, the righteous are described as possessing the character of a person who does the right thing rather than gratifying some immediate need. Who are they? "Those who lead blameless lives and do what is right, speaking the truth from sincere hearts. . . and who keep their promises even when it hurts" (Ps 15:2,4 NLT).

My father was always known as a man of his word. This I came to realize as I gleaned insights about him from those who knew him best. And in the small rural community in which he was born, lived his life and died, there was hardly anyone who did not know him well. People could depend upon him because he stood by his convictions in ways that were costly to him.

My first venture into farming for myself required that I go the local banker and ask for a loan. Not having any equity in property on which to guarantee the loan I was rather anxious about it. "Aren't you Albert Anderson's son," the banker asked? "Yes," I replied. He then placed a piece of paper in front of me and said, "How much do you need? If you are his son your signature is all the collateral I need to make this loan."

It was then that I discovered the moral legacy of character that my father had grown from the seed of his own kept promises, some of them, 'to his own hurt.' I did not have to 'start from scratch,' as it were, to build a foundation of honesty. His honesty was a legacy that could only be preserved by using it! Honesty is related more to character than to personality traits. And character is formed through the social structures in which self-identity is determined. We seldom 'start from scratch' in life, but emerge either with a substantial deposit or a significant deficit of character at our disposal. Those who have no legacy of honesty enter life with two strikes against them, and some with three.

All human relations are built on promises given and commitments made. Some are informal and so concealed in the structures of domestic and community life that we hardly realize they are there until they are broken. What makes promise-making difficult is that we never know in advance what it will cost to keep the promise. But that is why promises are expected. If it were always to our advantage and for our benefit to do something, there would be no need of promise-making.

There is an underlying fabric to life that binds all promises and commitments to a common source. This fabric is woven out of our convictions and gives assurance that the commitments and promises we make have the character of dependability about them.

Convictions can be costly. But until what we believe has been tested by the costliness of that belief, it is not a deep conviction. Our faith is confessed in terms of momentous events that God has done for us. We confess our faith and so honor God. Our convictions are expressed in the stand we take over sometimes trivial things for the sake of our own integrity.

Convictions are what make us dependable people when the temptation is to cut and run when the odds are against us or self-interest prevails. It is not where we take a stand that makes conviction a value, but that we **do** take a stand. It is not the importance of the issue or the magnitude of the battle that determines the character of a person. Heroism is not a character trait because one accomplishes a magnificent feat or loses one's life in a glorious battle. The test of conviction is in the ordinary affairs of life, not the extraordinary.

In the twilight of King David's life, the chronicler lists the names of the thirty 'mighty men,' David's warriors who gained renown through their heroic exploits. Some are simply named, while the deeds of three closest to David are noted as being worthy of remembering. The name of Shammah is listed as one of the three. The Israelites under David's leadership were gathered in battle against the Philistines "where there was a plot of ground full of lentils; and the army fled from the Philistines. But he took his stand in the middle of the plot, defended it, and killed the Philistines; and the Lord brought about a great victory" (2 Samuel 23:11-12; see also 1 Chronicles 11:12-13).

I will never forget the first time that I read this account! I was struck by the fact that this man's deed for which he was most remembered took place in the midst of a lentil field. This was apparently not by accident. We are told that he "took his stand in the middle of the plot, and defended it." Who owned the field we are not told. But it represented in the mind of this man not a small piece of the land he was sworn to defend but the entirety of it. To give up this small plot was to surrender something in his soul to the enemy. Do we confess our faith as the 'whole cloth" of our religion, but then often give it up in small pieces when convictions are sacrificed to the expediency of the moment?

Both the implicit and explicit commitments that comprise our life are thus pieces of the whole. If we give away one piece, we have rent the whole. Breaking one promise cannot be isolated from the whole of one's character. Each time a promise or commitment is broken, conviction as the core of character is pulled up by the roots and left to wither in the sun.

Character is the whole of our life and conviction is the stand we take on a small piece in which we defend the whole. The seed that produces character is often invisible, or even foolish to others. We know little else about this man, Shammah. He knew the difference between a seed and a need. The temptation is to think that our needs take precedence over our deeds. When we weigh the fruit that comes, we discover that the seed of conviction sown in season yields the character for which we hope. Hope is a costly grace. Like a grain of wheat, said Jesus, it produces nothing until it is sown in the ground, dies, and then yields its fruit (John 12:24).

Hope is Not a Fruit Unless it has a Seed

Every glorious harvest has its gloomy spring. Self-indulgence and self-gratification are late-sleepers but first at the table. "If wishes were horses then every beggar would ride," my mother used to say when I pestered her about wanting some toy to give me pleasure when I was bored. Even the fruit of the Spirit requires cultivation, while the desires of the flesh arise out of our passions, says the Apostle Paul. Love, joy, peace, kindness and gentleness are fruit, which means that each must have a seed and each be sown, cultivated and grown. Envy, strife, jealousy are always in season and instantly available (Gal 5:24).

Remember my friend, the financial advisor? He told me that many people just hope that things will work out so that they will have some degree of financial security when they retire without making the hard decisions now that will later determine future benefits. The answer he often receives when he asks whether a prospective client has the prospect of a good quality of life in retirement is, "Well I hope so." That's not good enough. Hope by itself produces nothing. Hope is not a virtue but it is the fruit of virtue. If hope is a fruit it must have a seed. And the seeds that produce hope are known by their fruit. A tree is known by its fruit, said Jesus (Mt 12:33). And so is the seed!

For example, if I want to plant a vegetable garden, I do not go to the market to compare one seed with another but I look for a packet of seeds that has a picture of the particular vegetable, such as a carrot, or a tomato, on its cover. It's no use trying to look at a seed and guess what kind of fruit that it will bear, unless one is an expert with regard to seeds. I know what an orange looks like but I am not sure that I could pick out an orange seed from a bowl of tangerine seeds. I trust that the seed will produce what the picture on the cover represents. Here is where faith is involved with hope. I have faith in the one who packaged the seeds. And so I trust that if planted in the ground to die that it will germinate and produce the kind of fruit promised. Faith does not have seeds, but hope does. But the seed of hope, without the faith invested in its cultivation, lies dormant. And faith without the seed of hope is utter vanity, and "a chasing after wind" (Eccl 1:14). So it is that in the case of hope we look first for what is hoped for and then for the seed that will yield that fruit.

How do we determine the difference between a need and a seed? Even here we must make a distinction between a present and future need. A future need, financial security, for example, is something that we hope for, and thus look for the seeds that will produce that benefit. An immediate need, even while necessary for our survival, such as for food, can be plucked from a tree that someone else has planted and cultivated. We consume it for our immediate gratification, which might be well and good if that was its intended use. But when we use our needs to feed on other people's seeds, we may experience immediate gratification but suffer spiritual malnutrition.

We emerge from the womb with instincts of self-gratification which others are prepared to serve, assuming the presence of normal care giving. Self-gratification requires neither hope nor faith, it is a need that is recognized as a form of health in the very young. But self-gratification is a need that not only does not allow for hope, it can devour the seed of hope before it has a chance to germinate and grow. Even as the weeds growing in a field of wheat compete for the nutrients and moisture in the soil

and threaten the existence of the harvest, self-gratification is a need that
shows no mercy to the tender and vulnerable seeds of hope. This is why
the preparation phase in hope is so important. The seed of hope also has
to do with the self. Hope offers self-fulfillment, not mere self-gratification.
But self-fulfillment requires preparation and perseverance in the face of
the incessant demands of self-gratification. Because the needs are there
before the seed, the sifting process must precede the sowing. This requires
what I would call 'spiritual intelligence.' The spirit that makes us human
gains its wisdom and strength through the Spirit that God gives to us.

The Spiritual Power of Everyday Life.

The move toward self-fulfillment rather than mere self-gratification
arises out of the spiritual core of our being rather than the physical. The
longing to be loved, to be valued, and to realize 'good reward' for our
toil is a sign that the spirit is alive with its own hunger. "Blessed are those
who hunger and thirst for righteousness, for they will be filled," said
Jesus (Mt 5:6). This is a hunger for 'goodness' that never diminishes in
'being filled,' for hope is the 'filling' that never makes us full. "For if we
already have something," said Paul, "We don't need to hope for it. But if
we look forward to something we don't yet have, we must wait patiently
and confidently" (Rom 8:24-25 NLT). Needs may be primarily physical
and emotional, and thus subject to immediate gratification, or frustration.
The emotional and physical aspects of our needs are brought under the
discipline of hope as we gain maturity as spiritual beings.

The preparation that goes into hope is the beginning of spiritual
wisdom as much as it is practical common sense. James, whose letter
is considered to be virtually a tract of practical wisdom, says that bitter
envy and selfish ambition do not emerge from God's wisdom that comes
down from above, but is "earthly, unspiritual and devilish" (James 3:15).
The wisdom from God is "pure, peaceable, gentle, willing to yield, full
of mercy and good fruits" (3:17). One does not hope to become a person
who is angry, spiteful, jealous and mean. These attributes come naturally
to one who allows self-gratification to be the primary passion in life. Our
better angels, as some have put it, awaken in us the longing to be good
(righteous) rather than evil. As James tells us, God 'planted' within us the
seed that was intended to bear the fruit of likeness to his own character.
"In fulfillment of his own purpose he gave us birth by the word of truth,
so that we would become a kind of first fruits of his creatures" (1:18). This
is the spiritual seed of hope.

While hope is singular as a spiritual quality of the soul, the fruit of
hope can only be gained as a specific goal. The German philosopher,

Martin Heidegger, told the story of a man who entered a market with a sign on the front, "Fruit for Sale." He asked for a pound of fruit. "I am sorry," the shopkeeper replied, " You cannot purchase a pound of fruit." The customer protested, "But you have a sign that says Fruit for Sale." The shopkeeper explained, "We do not have fruit. You cannot buy fruit. We do have apples, oranges, and pears. You can buy some of them, but as for fruit, it does not exist and cannot be purchased." When we give names for that which is only an abstract concept, we have not yet 'tasted' the reality. The reality of hope produces the image of hope. This is the first lesson in the wisdom of hope.

The seed of hope comes with a picture of the fruit of hope. The Apostle Paul had the picture in his mind when he wrote, "I have fought the good fight, I have finished the race, I have kept the faith. From now on there is reserved for me the crown of righteousness, which the Lord, the righteous judge, will give me on that day, and not only to me but also to all who have longed for his appearing" (2 Tim 7-8). He does not mention hope, but how else would you describe that which gave him direction, courage and faith through the twists and turns of his life, other than hope? To receive the crown of a righteous person, to belong to the congregation of the righteous (Ps 1:5), this was the vision of hope that inspired his faith. So what then is the seed? It is longing—"to all who have longed for his appearing."

The Seed of Longing

It is not enough to long to be with God; we might hope for that. But such a hope lacks a seed that we can plant, nourish and cultivate into a fruit. Being a righteous person is the fruit of longing, not a product of our making. The Psalmist draws the picture for the seed packet of hope. A righteous person is like a tree planted by living water, bearing its fruit in its season. Its leaves do not wither. "And in all they do, they prosper" (Ps 1:3).

I long to be that person. I want to "hunger and thirst for righteousness" (Mt 5:6). I aspire, like Job, to be described by God at the very outset as "a blameless and upright [righteous] man who fears God and turns away from evil" (Job 1:8). You have to have the seed of longing in your soul to be that righteous person. Paul, like Job, suffering senseless loss and pain, caught in his own self-boasting, nonetheless longed for what he looked for—the crown of righteousness. This is righteousness without religion. It is a lifetime achievement reward that finally reveals the fruit of the Spirit embodied in everyday life.

Gerald May wrote that we are to befriend our yearning rather than try to avoid it. We need to experience the "spaciousness of our emptiness," rather than trying to fill it up with activities and consumables. He says: "Emptiness, yearning, incompleteness: these unpleasant words hold a hope for incomprehensible beauty. It is precisely in these seemingly ab-horrent qualities of ourselves—qualities that we spend most of our time trying to fix or deny—that the very thing we most long for can be found: hope for the human spirit, freedom for love. This is a secret known by those who have had the courage to face their own emptiness."

If the longing is in your soul, it is the seed planted by God's own Spirit. Thus the fruit of righteousness is vibrant, colorful, alive and prosperous. I have to keep that picture before me to keep the longing alive in my heart. It is that picture, that moment, when the blessing of God rests upon my head, that stirs my longing and causes it to burst out of the soil and grow like a tender plant in what is often the crazy weed-patch of my life. But, as the Psalmist says, "I bless the Lord who gives me counsel; in the night my heart instructs me. I keep the Lord always before me; because he is at my right hand I will not be moved" (Ps 16:7-8).

This is the picture that identifies the seed of hope for me. Now I must, in my imagination, turn to the 'fanning mill' in order to separate out that seed from the needs that demand their own part of my soul. I think that I have the right seed. Now I need to do some work on the soil.

Chapter 2 - Tilling

Loosening the Soil so That it Can Breathe

When Thelma (not her real name), a middle-aged woman, came for pastoral counseling she sat down and without waiting for me to speak said, "I am a survivor. I have been through a lot and I can make it through this time as well. I just need to talk about it and then get on with life." I waited. Her hands were tightly clasped in her lap. What would otherwise have been a slight smile on her face was more of a grimace as her set jaw tensed the muscles in her cheeks.

As it turned out she did need to talk. But as she did, it became clear that the words were being used to suppress a deep pain and sadness in her heart instead of giving voice to a deeper inarticulate part of her self. Scripture verses and spiritual insights were liberally sprinkled throughout her conversation, but they puddled without really sinking in, like rain on a pathway hardened by the foot traffic of daily routine.

I had seen it before. A portion of a field on my father's farm never yielded a good harvest, even though the ground next to it produced a bumper crop. The rain fell as freely and fully on the unproductive soil as on the other. My father called the local county agricultural agent to come by and make an assessment of the unyielding soil. A small auger was inserted into the ground and the result was clear. "This portion of the field has a solid, impervious clay hardpan lying a few inches underneath the top soil," he reported. "The seeds will sprout and begin to grow, but the roots cannot go deep enough to draw upon the underlying moisture. In fact," he said, "no amount of rain will produce any crop on that soil because the hardpan will not permit the water to soak through. You need to break up that hardpan if you want anything to grow in this soil. You have got to loosen up that hardpan and allow the soil to 'breathe' in order to grow a plant to maturity."

Well, we had always plowed that portion of the field down to the normal depth of about 6 inches as with the rest of the field before planting.
From the surface of the soil there appeared to be no difference. What was
needed was not just to set the plow a bit deeper, but to bring in a 'chisel'
type of implement to rip up the hardpan to a depth of at least 18 inches.
This was accompanied by the working in of a liberal amount of organic
plant material in order to prevent the clay particles in the soil from bond-
ing and forming another hardpan. This is what is meant by tilling the soil,
not merely plowing it. The work was expensive and time consuming. But
it worked. The next planting on that portion of the field was done with
more hope, and the hope was realized in a better harvest.

As I listened to Thelma's overly-glib conversation and attempted to
deposit what I thought were insightful bits of wisdom in the spaces between her words, I began to see something of what I had observed in my
father's field—an impervious hardpan lying beneath the surface that even
she did not realize and which I could not penetrate. She said that she had
just come to talk. But I realized that some deeper work was necessary if
she were to discover the hope that she was looking for. I could walk and
talk with her on that old pathway, but the result would be only to harden
the soil and create some puddles of hope that would quickly evaporate in
the full sun of everyday life. If I probed beneath her defences this would
likely cause more pain than she was willing to bear. After all, she did not
come to experience more hurt, but to get over the most recent pain as
quickly as possible.

Those who are trained as therapists and counselors tell us that the
most difficult point in therapy is the point where a person feels the first
healing of superficial pain and then wants to 'get better' as quickly as
possible. Whereas, what is often needed is to probe into further pain in
order to produce a deeper healing and a hope that does not perish with
the next dry season. In other words to 'till the soil.'

The first session was coming to a close. "Why did you really come," I
asked, "And what do you long for the most?"

Now the tears came. The longing was the probe. Longing goes deeper
than pain, though it may also be the source of pain. Sealing off the pain,
stifles the longing. The longing still had no voice but it began to flow,
along with the tears. She came for the next session to find new words
for feelings that had for too-long been suppressed by rituals that never
brought renewal and promises that never yielded hope. Eventually she
not only found hope, but spiritual empowerment to do more than survive,
to recover and to live on the growing edge.

The analogy of the hardpan and the need to till the soil fits very well into this chapter's concern for preparation of the soil prior to planting the seed of hope. It also represents the problem of resistance to the word of the Kingdom as portrayed in Jesus' parable of the sower that is actually a parable of the different kinds of soil. While the seed that fell on good soil yielded a harvest of up to a hundredfold, the seed that fell on the hard rocky soil grew rapidly, but perished just as rapidly because the soil was shallow (Mt 13:18-23). There was no indication in the parable that one could dig deeper in the rocky soil and make it more suitable for yielding a more bountiful harvest. Yet the implication is there. One need not give up hope when the harvest is poor, rather one can recondition the soil. In another parable, Jesus told of a man who planted a fig tree in his vineyard but it did not produce fruit for three years. When the owner asked that it be cut down, the gardener protested and asked that it be given another year during which he would dig round it, recondition the soil, and see if it then could not produce. In other words, do not give up hope but do some soil preparation (Luke 13:6-9).

In the previous chapter I talked about the seed of longing. Longing for the good life, longing for self-fulfillment rather than yielding to self-gratification, this is the kind of longing that lies at the very core of the self. The seed of longing was placed in our soul by the Creator. It is one way of discovering within us the divine image. It is a frequent expression of the Psalmist. "As a deer longs for flowing streams, so my soul longs for you, O God" (Ps 42:1). Longing is vulnerable to unfulfilled hope and unanswered prayer. When that happens, a protective shield is often constructed to protect the seed of longing from the risk of another failed harvest. When longing is wounded, the seed of hope remains sterile and unsown.

How the Hardpan is Constructed

Longing is the first to be wounded when hope fails and the most difficult to heal. Most other wounds to the self heal with time, for they lie closer to the surface. When longing is deceived and hope is betrayed, the first response is to drive longing deeper into the self and the first line of defense against further hurt is to hide the longing lest it be hurt again. But hiding never heals. And unhealed longing solidifies into a clay-like substance within the soul. The result is a hardpan of mistrust mixed with bitterness; the hardpan does its work, but at great price to the soul of hope. The seed lies in darkness, fearful of the light, dormant, though still alive underneath the hardpan of impervious clay.

The effect of suffering, pain, and experience of loss upon the self is a narrowing one. Anxiety causes the self to tighten up. The Latin word for anxiety is *angustia*, a word that means narrowness. The flow of blood is restricted. Muscular movements become stiff and constricted. The self retreats into isolation and sets up defenses against the intrusion of further pain.

When the self experiences pain it takes a negative direction, pulling back from shock and refusing to deal with the change that comes about through unexpected events and sudden losses. The self attempts to restore its familiar sense of order by locating a known center that is secure and safe. This coping mechanism of withdrawal is sometimes the only defense left to a person suffering loss of hope. The self creates an inner refuge from the violence, much as a person living amidst urban terrorism places iron bars on the windows and cowers inside.

Persons who experience the devastating loss of a marriage or the death of a loved one often find it difficult to deal with the shock of losing something that had become so much a part of self-identity. Like an earthquake fault that splits one's house in two, a sudden and traumatic loss is a seismic shudder that can cause the self to retreat from the fault line of pain in order to stop the tremors. "The human spirit will endure sickness; but a broken spirit—who can bear" (Prov 18:14).

With brokenness there is bleeding. Every hurt and each loss is a hemorrhage through which the self bleeds its pain. Left to ourselves, we attempt to staunch the flow as best we can. After a time, the wound seems to be healed and the pain subsides. Then suddenly a tremor arises within us and the hurt spills over again, an embarrassment to us and a discomfort for others. Healed over pain is like a hidden land mine, one misstep and it blows up right in our face. We should never walk alone in the pathway of recovery. We need companions who have walked that way before and who are safe escorts.

Some might think of emotional trauma and pain as a state of disorder in the self. Actually, emotional pain in a dysfunctional relationship constitutes the most stable of all systems, and least susceptible to change. To introduce change into a rigid emotional structure of the self only stiffens the resistance. This is how the hardpan develops in the soil of the self.

Not all of us, as did Thelma who came to me for counseling, live with a hardpan beneath the surface that hides our deepest longings and protects the seed of hope from another failure. But sooner or later, we all suffer from the failure of hope and need to replant. When that happens, there may be some digging to do before we sow the seed. The key word for Thelma was not just longing, but what do you long for *most*. We all have levels of longing, some are quite superficial, others lie deeper in the self. But there is in each of us a longing for ultimate meaning and fulfillment. It may at times be attached to some one or some thing that crosses our path.

Longing loves to live in the imagination, but it also can wither and die there. The seed of hope is such a longing, and it must be released in order that hope can be envisioned and grasped by faith.

The Breakthrough to Longing

Growth toward wholeness and the renewal of hope cannot begin until self-deception and self-justification are broken and the self experiences a vulnerability that creates an opening through which real contact with others can occur. The most difficult movement for the self to make in digging deeper is to experience a real breakdown in the defenses that enabled one to survive as a victim. This 'break-through' often leaves a broken edge that should not be covered over quickly. The broken edge needs to become a growing edge. The breaking of the self's survival skills in the face of pervasive failure and punishing loss is a broken edge which is most painful of all. This is the broken edge, however, where the spirit of renewal and recovery can heal and lead to growth.

In the parable of the Prodigal Son, the son was not broken in spirit by the desperate conditions in the far country where he was reduced to living with the swine. He returned home with a confession upon his lips but with no joy in his heart. He thought that his life as a son was finished for good, and he was prepared to live in his father's house as a servant. Instead, the father rushed out and kissed him, and proclaimed, "This son of mine was dead and is alive again; he was lost and is found" (Luke 15:24)!

The broken edge was not due solely to the son's failure to achieve what he set out to do, but to the damaged relationship which only the father could restore. The human spirit is nurtured by relationship not by rules. When we break the rules we suffer the consequences. When we experience a broken relationship we suffer a brokenness of spirit. The broken edge of the relationship with the father became a creative opportunity for the son to become what he had not yet achieved--a life of sonship with an openness to the future. It was there at the broken edge that the growing edge of recovery and restoration began. Restoration is the recovery of the spiritual power of our lives to become the person that God intended.

The spiritual dimension for hope begins where the broken edge becomes the growing edge. All brokenness brings emotional pain for which there is no rational relief. The healing of emotional pain is the spiritual work of the self. Growth does not come through emotional change alone but through the life of the spirit. It is the spirit that expands the self and directs the self toward growth. The feelings of the self are the core of

subjectivity and individuality. The spirit of the self constitutes the openness of the self to the spirit of others and, essentially and ultimately to
the Spirit of God.

The brokenness of the human spirit is a deeper and more creative edge
than mere guilt and remorse for sin. A sense of guilt is not creative and
produces no positive motivation toward spiritual wholeness. There is no
need to make people whose spirit is broken feel condemned as a condition for receiving grace. In fact, this may well bruise the broken spirit and
turn what could be a hopeful spiritual experience of recovery of the joy
of salvation into a hopeless inward spiral of self-condemnation. We tend
to forget that the cross of Christ only has significance as a place where
sin is judged for those who have experienced the power of resurrection
and the gift of the Spirit of God.

It is the spiritual core of the self that gives direction to the emotions
and expands the creative capacity of the self. When the irrepressible spirit
of creativity, imagination and vision is unleashed within us, we move
away from the security of a fixed center toward the growing edge. It is our
spiritual life of faith, hope and love that enables the self to transcend its
boundaries, to move beyond its own history, and create its new story.

A healthy self is one that is in balance and capable of growth. If traumatic shock and grievous loss has produced emotional rigidity—it is the
self's desperate attempt to maintain balance and control under trauma
and stress. A growing self is dynamic and flexible, able to absorb shock,
to make adjustments under stress, and to shift the center of gravity of the
self in order to maintain balance.

When we merely survive by retreating from the broken edge in search
of a space that is under control and not subject to change, we hide the seed
of longing behind an impervious hardpan. Change must be introduced as
a challenge to recover hope. The paradox is that change is a break in the
established pattern and produces momentary disequilibrium in the rigid
structure of the self. Before change and growth can occur, the structure
of the self must shift from a rigid to a dynamic and flexible state. This
requires a strongly supportive environment so that sufficient balance and
stability is provided for the self while experiencing the stress and 'shifting
of the ground' under one's feet.

Openness to the spirit of others and to supportive relationships is
crucial to a process of growth and change. The recovery of hope means
the recovery of the self in relationship, sustained by a spiritual openness
to love, faith and hope. This is the recovery of the original form of the self
as created in the image and likeness of God.

Releasing the Longing

The first step is to overcome the effects of the constriction of the self that produced the hardpan and to emerge into the larger space of self-expression where longing again emerges in the heart and hope looms on the horizon. This means that one must go beyond mere survival and go deeper in order to go further. To think of ourselves as survivors may feel empowering to the self emotionally and enable us to function to some degree, but it fails to satisfy the deeper yearnings and possibilities of the self. Growth toward full restoration of creative life builds on the overcoming of the constricting force of anxiety produced by suffering and pain. Overcoming a crisis can be like crawling out of a raging river gorge that threatens to carry us downstream to our destruction. Having escaped the force of the stream that seeks to pull us under, we have become a survivor.

Survival is a powerful instinct of self, but it may not yet offer hope. Survivors may have conquered an addiction, learned to let go of a tragic loss, escaped from dysfunctional relationships and be healed of traumatic abuse, but this is still not enough. The deep feelings experienced during intense pain and suffering may actually be a narrowing of the flow of emotions by denying the full range of feelings which contribute to the health and creative life of the self. The goal is not to emerge from an abusive relationship or traumatic experience as a battle-scarred survivor but as a passionate lover of life and full of hope. Beyond overcoming is becoming. More than emotional repair is needed. We have not fully recovered until there is restored the abundant spiritual life of fellowship with God and relation with others. Restoration is the fullness of God creating a new a spiritual dimension.

Perhaps we have never experienced this fullness. Or, we have only experienced the longing for it. Each of us has the God-given capacity for becoming what we were created to be. Even our unfulfilled longing is a witness to this capacity. Recovery of hope begins with opening up this capacity and then moving us toward fulfillment. This is the experience of God's gracious Spirit working with our spirit.

With Thelma, I did not begin by attempting to dig deeper by beginning at the surface, as this would only have hardened the protective wall behind which her real, but wounded self lay. Instead, I spoke directly to that wounded self by naming it as longing. "What do you long for the most?" We are most vulnerable with respect to what we long for. But our deepest longing is also the most powerful seed of hope.

Longing is dangerous. It can act as a stimulant, speeding up our anticipation and lead to frustration when time and circumstances block fulfillment. Longing is an expression of love, but can never be the fulfillment of love. This is why longing is the seed of hope not its harvest. The peril of longing is that it makes us vulnerable to deception and sometimes the victim of betrayal. "When you search for me you will find me; if you seek me with all your heart" (Jer 29:13). This is an invitation to the greatest experience a human person can have, an encounter with God, "Blessed are the poor in heart, for they will see God" (Mt 5:8). Careful! That may be a fatal attraction for the longing that drives that search must be held by the hand of faith. "For we walk by faith and not by sight" (2 Cor 5:7).

There is thus a paradox in longing. To possess what we long for not only makes longing for it unnecessary, but in possessing it we no longer hope for it. "Now hope that is seen is not hope, . . . But if we hope for that which we do not see, we wait for it with patience" (Rom 8:24, 25).

The German pastor and theologian, Dietrich Bonhoeffer, became engaged to Maria von Wedemeyer (half his age!) just a few months before he was arrested in April of 1943 for his involvement in a conspiracy against Hitler. In May of 1944, just eleven months before his execution by Hitler in April of 1945, He wrote to Maria in response to her letter in which she had expressed great frustration and anxiety about their separation. His meditation on longing is profound and poignant, given the circumstances and setting, worth reprinting in full. Deprived of sharing his love through physical presence, she agonized and despaired over the situation. He wrote back:

> If our love were merely agonizing deprivation, we should probably die of unassuaged longing in our separate cages. There are already inherent in our love, not deprivation and desire alone, but-miraculously enough--the beginnings of fulfillment. I constantly cling to that, and my gratitude for it is such that what already exists is far more important to me than what is still to come. The latter is as certain to come about in its own good time as the former, and then all will be fulfilled more and more. Our longing for each other is great, to be sure, but it will grow steadily greater the more we are together and fulfill our togetherness. Isn't love always, but always, a mutual longing that can never be fully assuaged? What would fulfillment be worth if it robbed us of that longing? It would spell the end of love, not its beginning, its essence, its consummation. But this mutual longing mustn't always connote frenzy and insensate desire, it mustn't always afflict and torment us, it needn't be forever fretting over what is still denied us. It should surely be like one's longing for a glorious spring morning, when one

sees the sky already tinged with red by the sun's first rays. It means waiting, desiring, and yearning, assuredly, but doing so with happiness and utter certainty. That's what our love is like, I believe, and it's all the better for being so.

Was he offering false hope by encouraging her to 'yearn' for a future with 'utter certainty?' What certainty could he offer her other than the 'certainty of hope?' By this time he was certainly well aware that his fate was virtually sealed by Hitler's knowledge of his involvement in the conspiracy to kill him. What hope can there be behind prison walls, for those outside as well as those within? Actually, he did not view physical separation as hopeless, as long as there was longing. Maria had imprisoned hope, as it were, within her own need and desperation. Her longing was not a seed of hope but a bitter pill of despair. By hoping out of desperation and need, she was already caught in the snare of false hope. In a passage that borders on divine inspiration he told her, "Isn't love always, but always, a mutual longing that can never be fully assuaged? What would fulfillment be worth if it robbed us of that longing?"

Could we but grasp the truth of that, love would not so easily be diminished by proximity and crushed in our own embrace. Nothing is less certain than that which we hold in our arms. As he embraced Eve for the first time, Adam cried out, "This, at last, is bone of my bones and flesh of my flesh" (Gen 2:23). The cloudless skies and moonless nights of longing were over, he thought. What her thoughts were, we will never know, except that when longing is removed from love it seeks a home in desire. Longing is not itself a temptation, but only when it is transformed into desire. It was so in the beginning, the story tells us. When Eve saw that the forbidden tree was "to be desired to make one wise, she took of its fruit and ate; and she also gave some to her husband" (Gen 3:6).

What Dietrich discovered in prison through hope delayed, if not also denied, is that longing is the seed that keeps love from dying, even in the proximity of desire's embrace. When Jesus said that the blessed are those who "hunger and thirst for righteousness, for they will be filled," (Mt 5:6), he surely meant us to understand that the 'filling' does not quench the thirst, but only causes it to become a deeper and devout longing that is itself the bond of love that binds us to God. The story of the first temptation is not the end of longing, but only the fruitlessness of desire. But desire cannot kill longing, it can only cause it to retreat, chagrined and shamed, cowering in the 'trees of the garden' and wearing the fig leaves whose covering is more of a confession than a concealment. Can longing live again?

Resowing the Seed of Longing

The only healing for the wounded seed of hope is for it to be resown. For this to happen, following the analogy of the soil, the hardpan must be penetrated and opened up. But this can only be done from the inside. At this point the analogy fails. There is no 'chisel' that breaks through from the outside, one must speak to the seed itself. Because the seed of hope is placed within us by the Spirit of God, the life of the seed responds to the Word of the Spirit. Jesus told his disciples, "The words that I have spoken to you are spirit and life" (John 6:63). Tilling, however, is different from merely digging. Tilling is an active stirring of the soil, mixing organic material with the clinging clay particles, opening up spaces between the elements so that air and water can filtrate through the soil, providing an environment for the seeds to germinate and the first growth to appear. Here is where the tilling of the soil, to follow the analogy, must do its work.

When brokenness occurs, as it does to all of us, it presents a crisis to the self. Openness to change is a characteristic of the self where the hardpan of denial is penetrated from underneath by longing. This is a work of the spirit, not of the will. The reach of the human spirit to the Spirit of God underlies the self's capacity for faith, hope and ultimately trust and acceptance. God's love issues from the heart of his longing. Jesus expressed this longing when he gathered his disciples for the last meal. "I have been very eager to eat this Passover with you before my suffering begins" (Luke 22:15 NLT). The spiritual dimension of hope is not a religious feeling toward God but a stirring of the human spirit under the tender caress of divine love. But divine love comes to us through other humans. It is not enough to ask, Who loves me? I need to know, Who longs for me? Who yearns to be my friend? Who has included me in their 'hope chest?' *The Heart is a Lonely Hunter*, wrote Carson Mcullers in a book that became a first run movie. The lead character who can neither hear nor speak, befriends others, but the seed of longing in his heart finds no one who longs for him. Being the object of indifferent love is not to be loved with longing.

Here we discover the double bind in the recover of hope. Without the supportive and affirming experience of others we walk alone like lonely survivors in a crowd. At the same time, it is often from those whom we have trusted and those to whom we have looked for support that we have received injury and abuse.

Life in relation to others is no protection against abuse, pain and tragic loss. In fact, shared promises and commitments raises the stakes of our losses and griefs. There is something in us that wants to avoid this by withholding commitment and preserving our independence. But solitariness (not solitude!) is a form of abuse for the human spirit. And walking alone provides no certainty of never falling. "Two are better than one, " wrote the ancient Preacher, "because they have a good reward for their toil. For if they fall, one will lift up the other; but woe to one who is alone and falls and does not have another to help" (Eccl 4:9-10). The seed of hope cannot germinate in darkness. There is no harvest of hope without breaking through the hardpan. Some have found this possible in spite of what appeared once to be the death of hope.

Anne Morrow Lindberg, after the tragic kidnapping and death of her son went through this process and finally discovered that the seed of longing, though hidden behind closed doors, could only find a harvest of hope when resown.

For Whom
The milk ungiven in the breast
When the child is gone?

For whom
The love locked up in the heart
That is left alone?

That golden yield
Split sod once, overflowed an August field,
Threshed out in pain upon September's floor,
Now hoarded high in barns, a sterile store.

Break down the door;
Rip open, spread and pour
The grain upon the barren ground
Wherever crack in clod is found.

There is no harvest for the heart alone;
The seed of love must be
Eternally Resown.

There are people who have walked the road to recovery and who have been restored. These are the ones with whom we can find our escorts for our own journey. When we experience brokenness within a community of support and care, there is an interchange, a transfusion, if you please, so that what life flows out of us flows back into us, filtered through the fabric of intentional care. Within the life of the self in relation to others, there flows the pain of others as well as the joy of others. Shared longing is the seed of hope. Longing is the spiritual power of willing. It is time to sow the seed.

Chapter 3 - Sowing

You Have to Will it, Not Just Want It

Edye Smith's face on the television screen was a tormented image of silent despair and grief. Her two young children, Chase, 3, and Colton, 2, had died in the bombing of the federal building in Oklahoma City early in 1995. Silently weeping, clutching two teddy bears, the camera captured the pathetic image at the nationally televised memorial service.

Some weeks later, in response to a reporter's question as to how she managed to face life with hope and optimism following the loss, Edye replied: "It is my faith that keeps me going," she responded. "Without faith in God I don't know how I could live through this loss and rebuild my life." When this same woman some months later had a surgical operation allowing her to conceive again so that she might have other children, television reporters called it a "miracle of faith."

The reporter's comment was not prompted by the surgery that reversed a previous tubal ligation. It was her vision of having more children, reuniting with her estranged husband and the beginning of a new life that evoked the response, "a miracle of faith." The medical marvel is a product of technology and science. The human spirit is not so easily re-manufactured when it has been broken. Nor is there any procedure for transplanting hope. It must emerge again from the place where it died.

One morning, Edye arose and looked out through the window of her soul and saw a vision of what God could create through her. Her anguished spirit brushed the face of God, and her spirit revived. "Without faith in God I don't know how I could have lived through this loss and rebuild my life." A miracle of faith and a re-birth of hope.

Three years later, on January 12, 1998, Edye gave birth to their son, Glenn. "When we took Chase and Colton's beds out of their room, I was crying and so sad," says Edye's mother, Kathy Wilburn, "But as we set up Glenn's bed that day, there was as new spirit of hope and joy."

Resowing the Seed of Hope

We cannot help but admire persons who survive difficult ordeals without collapsing into self-pity and bitterness. How does one sow the seed of hope again in the face of adversity and tragic loss? Is hope a spiritual gift to the chosen few, or is it a resource which each one of us has at our disposal if only we could find the key?

The person whose faith goes no further than making a confession of faith in God does not attract our attention as much as one who lives out faith with vision and commitment. We admire the virtue of faith when its vision leads to victory in the struggle of life. The woman who suffered the loss of her children turned away from the gaping hole and rubble in which her children died to envision new life out of death. She found within herself the seed of longing that envisioned bearing another child. Hope came alive amidst the barren ruins of hopelessness.

Psychologists might question the motivation for her action, searching for evidences that she has not dealt with her loss in a healthy way and is seeking to 'replace' her loss rather than accept it. They might also be concerned that she somehow feels responsible for not preventing this horrible tragedy and that she is now seeking to atone for her guilt. But such a psychological analysis does not account for the spiritual power of hope that became a will to act in order to bring a vision into reality.

The spiritual dimension of hope is the capacity of the self to envision a harvest following a devastating loss. This leads to convictions that translate into actions. It is not enough to want to reap a new harvest, one must have the will to till the soil and plant the seed. This is faith at work so that hope does not remain a sterile seed. Faith at work is apparently more pleasing to God than faith at rest. The profession of faith is fine, wrote James, but what good is it without works? "Even the demons believe," James reminded his readers. For James, faith that didn't work was of no practical value. While others made great claims to faith, James countered, "By my works I will show you my faith" (James 2:18-19). James appears to be giving us an early version of the more recent Twelve Step admonition that change will not occur until we 'walk the talk.'

We often refer to Abraham when we think of faith, but not of Sarah when we speak of hope. Abraham 'wanted' to have a son and came to God with his complaint (Genesis 15:3). God promised him a son without explaining how this might be accomplished despite the fact that his wife was not only barren but now beyond the age of child-bearing. Sarah understood this and took herself out of the process by suggesting that if

Abraham wanted a son he could have one by taking her servant maid, Hagar, as a surrogate mother. As a result Hagar gave birth to Abraham's son, Ishmael. True, it was Abraham's seed but not the seed of hope based on the promise. Thirteen years later, when Abraham is now one hundred years old and Sarah is approaching ninety, God reminds Abraham that he has not forgotten his promise. "I will give you a son by her," God told him, which caused Abraham to fall on his face with laughter and exclaim, "Can Sarah who is ninety years old bear a child?" (Genesis 17:15-17). For Abraham, the promise had already been fulfilled despite the hopelessness of Sarah's condition. "O that Ishmael might live in your sight!" But the Lord said, no, you must embrace the barrenness of Sarah with hope and together bring forth the promised son.

The biblical story goes no further, but I do. I want to know what Sarah said when Abraham approached her with this 'Word of the Lord.' After all, it was not Abraham's faith that was the seed of hope; that had been sown and produced a son that was set aside. Sarah is the one who has to take up hope again in order for Abraham's faith to bring forth the promise of God. Why are we so preoccupied with faith that we forget about the importance of hope? I think that it is because in our minds, faith seems easier and hope appears more difficult. The seed of hope is longing. Abraham does not long for a child as Sarah must have. He only complains that he has none and makes out of his complaint an argument to God. In the face of the obstacle of Sarah's barrenness, faith takes the easier route of finding a more fertile soil in which to plant his seed.

"We have to turn toward each other again, and embrace your barrenness with the hope that this time you will conceive," Abraham tells his wife. "You have no right to ask this of me," she replies, "Thank God for the day in which there was no longer a possibility to conceive. All those years I lived with hope that I could conceive, but that hope died a thousand deaths. At last I could accept my barrenness as my fate and let go of hope. I can accept being barren, it has become a comfort to me. No one, not even God can blame me for not conceiving. Now you are asking me to hope again. I don't think I can bear it."

I have no biblical text in support of this dialogue of course. But do I really need one? Would not a woman read the same story quite differently than a man? While theologians extol the faith of Abraham (yes, the biblical authors do as well), one cannot narrate the emergence of hope out of barrenness without the story of Sarah. Her consent is more than submission to a physical act as part of her marital duty. She has to allow the seed of longing to emerge behind the hardpan of resignation to her fate in order for it to break through and bear a child of promise. This is more than wanting a child, it is being willing to sow the seed of hope in soil that even faith has passed over as hopeless. Only Sarah can tell us of how difficult it is to hope, and only from Sarah can faith learn to go beyond wanting something from God and conceiving something from God. Conceiving is an act of hope, by which faith works to receive the promise and gift of God.

The compelling factor in the case of the woman with which I began this chapter is the fact that it was a woman, not a man, who grasped hope so securely that it led her to undergo a procedure that enabled her to conceive again. What more could she do? The seed of hope begins with longing, a vision that could only be fulfilled by 'tilling the soil,' breaking up the hardpan of bitter grief, and making it physically possible to conceive. She is Sarah. Her husband, in this story, remained nameless. Yes it was a miracle, but she willed the miracle by sowing the seed of hope.

This is why I am writing about hope and not just about faith. James says that faith without works is dead (James 2:17). I paraphrase that to say that faith without hope is impotent.

There is No Harvest Without a Sowing

Nature tells us that it is futile to attempt by faith to grow a crop when the seed has never been sown. This is common sense to one who tills the soil. It matters little how long and hard one prays in faith for a bountiful crop when the seed has never been planted. It is an old joke, but makes a good point. A man stood up in church and prayed that he would win the lottery and would give 10% to the church. When he did not win, he again prayed, more fervently than ever and added that he would now be willing to give 50% to the church. When that failed, he prayed loudly to the Lord demanding to know why his prayer was not answered. Suddenly there was a booming voice echoing throughout the church, "This is the Lord, buy a ticket." End of joke, no sequel.

The point is that it is not enough to want something from God and then wait for God to drop it in our laps. That is not just common sense, it is spiritual wisdom. Without the act of sexual intercourse between Abraham and his barren wife, Sarah, there would be no child. While the birth of Isaac was a miracle of divine grace, it was not faith alone that produced the child but the willingness of both to 'partner' with God through their own actions.

Faith asks, what are you willing to believe? Hope asks, what are you willing to do? What are you willing to invest for the sake of reaping a harvest? When hope arises as a longing rather than merely as a wanting, and when the longing becomes a vision of what God can do, the seed must be sown so that faith is grounded in reality not fantasy. The author of the book of Hebrews defines faith as "the assurance of things hoped for, the conviction of things not seen" (Hebrews 11:1). It is important to note that 'things not seen' are, by definition, invisible though still 'things.' The assurance on which faith rests is not always visible, though it is very real. What is often missed in this text is the reference to "things hoped for." It is hope that requires a seed to be sown so that faith has the basis for a conviction that the unseen vision of hope is real, not a fantasy.

This is the difference between faith and folly. Folly is the attempt to 'make visible what is unreal and so elicit commitment from others and give oneself permission to satisfy greed and grandiosity. Folly manufactures evidence where there is none, while faith sees evidence that is not visible. In retrospect, the difference becomes quite clear. Faith envisions what is real, though not visible, while folly makes visible what is unreal. Folly may be likened to the weeds which grow amidst the wheat, appearing at early stages to be quite similar. It is only at harvest, said Jesus, that the wheat can be separated as it has produced a full head of grain (Mt 13:24-30).

One might address the woman in Oklahoma City from a faith perspective and ask: "Are you willing to believe that God can enable you to conceive a child and that through faith alone what is impossible from a scientific perspective is possible from God's perspective?" This would be to pray for a harvest without sowing the seed.

On the other hand, from a hope perspective one might ask her: "Are you willing to do what is necessary in order for you to recover your natural ability to conceive and give birth to a child?" This, in fact, is what she did by undergoing the medical procedure (tilling the soil) in order to plant the seed, and receive as a gift from God that for which she longed.

Please do not misunderstand me. I am not attempting to play off hope against faith; they are symbiotic aspects of a healthy spiritual life where the temporal and the eternal, heaven and earth, are joined in a seamless reality where one dissolves into the other. At the same time, both hope and faith have their own function and role to play. I fear that hope is often viewed as a more ephemeral and unsubstantial, even mystical aspect of our faith life. While on the other hand, faith is viewed as a way to 'get something' from God without putting in much of our own effort, as though that would undermine its authenticity.

Caught off guard by Jesus' insistence that forgiveness is a moral duty rather than a spiritual option, the disciples blurt out, "Show us how to increase our faith" (Luke 17:5 NLT). In a way that was typical of Jesus' response, he turned the situation around and said that it was not a matter of getting more faith, but using the little that they had, even as small as a mustard seed, it could uproot and throw a tree into the ocean (17:6).

Faith, by itself is always an 'impossible' approach to life. If faith were concerned with what is possible from a human point of view, it would not be faith but merely pragmatism—belief in what works. If it doesn't work then faith has failed, or we 'need more faith.' When we link faith to God we are immediately dealing with what is impossible. This is what Jesus does in telling his disciples that even a small faith can move a mountain, or throw a tree into the ocean. The disciples think that by having larger faith they could enlarge possibility, but that is simply a pragmatic approach, making faith work for us. Those who use faith in that way are closer to the realm of magic than mystery.

I have little confidence in a 'faith approach' to farming. One could stand forever in front of a barren piece of land and pray in faith for a good crop without ever having to invest in harvest equipment. But one who sows in hope better make some arrangements for the harvest, and then have faith that it will be needed! I think that this is why James says concerning the faith of Abraham: "His actions made his faith complete" (James 2:22 NLT). Hope is attached to something we long for, it is an investment of some part of ourselves in that which life and love holds for us in store. Why that longing is already and always fulfillment, as Bonhoeffer reminded us in the previous chapter, is a mystery. Faith lives in the mystery of hope so that with God 'all things are possible.' In this way, faith embraced by hope, never fails. Faith only fails when it stands alone. The seed of hope as 'the work of love,' and the harvest of hope as the 'completion of faith,' rests in the mystery of the divine promise. In this way "We know that all things work together for good" (Rom 8:28).

Given a choice between two churches, one on either side of the street, one called Faith Church and other Hope Church, I think that I know which one I would want to enter. Fortunately I don't have to make that choice being a member of Grace church where both hope and faith are alive and well and my Sunday morning adult class meets in Hope Hall!

The Season for Sowing

The metaphors of sowing and reaping were favorite with the apostle Paul. Applied with respect to the flesh and the spirit he warned, "You reap whatever you sow" (Gal 6:7). This has more to do with hope than faith. The 'works of the flesh' as Paul described them, are the result of passion, self-ambition and are destructive to the self and others (Gal 5:19-21). In contrast, sowing to the Spirit results in the fruit of the Spirit, qualities of life that are personally enriching and promote the wellbeing of others (Gal 5:22-26). But when and how do we sow to the Spirit? How do we apply these creative metaphors to our own daily lives?

First, there is as time and a season for both sowing and reaping. "For everything there is a season, and time for every matter under heaven" (Ecc 3:1). If this is true in nature it may also hold true for our personal and spiritual life. One ordinarily thinks of spring as the time for sowing and Fall as the time for reaping. That is basically true where the four seasons prevail as in South Dakota where I grew up and operated my own farm. But strangely enough there was an exception. We had the choice between raising what we called spring wheat and winter wheat. Winter wheat was a variety of wheat that could survive the cold winter and be ready to continuing growing with the first warm days of spring. Spring wheat was only sown after the frozen ground had thawed and was warm enough to sow the wheat seeds.

There were risks with both options. If the winter wheat did not have a strong enough growth before winter set in, it could be damaged during the winter. On the other hand, spring was often late in arriving and the spring wheat could not be planted in time and so a poor harvest was the result. For those not initiated into the process, it seemed utter folly to prepare the soil and sow wheat in the fall when snow was likely to fall within a month or two. But for those who understand the 'seasons' and the nature of wheat, if conditions were favorable, sowing winter wheat made a lot of sense. With some fall rains after the sowing, the wheat germinated, and the plants grew to about three or four inches before the frost came and the ground was frozen. One always hoped for some early fall rain and a late frost when sowing winter wheat! Faith in a good harvest depended upon getting the soil prepared and the sowing done in 'good time.'

One of the more poignant verses in the Bible is found in Jeremiah 8:20, "The harvest is past, the summer is ended, and we are not saved." Something has gone wrong. The growing season is over, the harvest was lost, winter is approaching, what hope is there? For those who only know about spring wheat, the answer is clear. Nothing to do but wait through the long winter. But for those who know about winter wheat, there is another option. Start preparing the soil and begin sowing! Keep hope alive.

Was it winter or spring when the young mother in Oklahoma had her vision of having another child? The two graves of her only children were still fresh with flowers, and her heart torn with grief; she saw the winter of her grief coming and sowed a seed of hope. After the surgical procedure, reconciliation with her estranged husband, and the conception of another child, she waited for her 'winter wheat' to emerge in the spring and her longing fulfilled.

Yes, I know, psychotherapists will remind me that she needs to go though the grief process. But she has nine months to do that, time to go through the stages; denial, anger, bargaining, and finally acceptance. But through that process she already has sown the seed of hope and has allowed the deeper longing in her soul to become attached to an outcome that will, in its own way, bring healing. Grief-work without hope-work can leave one as barren as before.

When Eve lost her first son, Abel, because of Cain's act of murder, she not only experienced the first human death recorded, but her summer had ended, and winter was descending on her soul. Without any psychological commentary, the narrative simply records the fact, "Adam knew his wife again, and she bore a son, and named him Seth, for she said, 'God has appointed me another child instead of Abel, because Cain killed him'" (Gen 4:25). That's winter wheat. It has its own season for sowing.

While we ordinarily think of spring as the time for sowing, and it usually is, sooner or later we will each come to the point of grieving some loss, surviving some 'summer storm,' and face the fact that a long winter might be coming. These times are often viewed as producing a crisis of faith. We turn to Job and seek wisdom from his response to the calamities that fell on him and his family. We think that we find there a pattern for faith when he said, "Shall we receive good at the hand of God, not receive the bad" (Job 2:19).

This could be interpreted as the resignation of faith. But throughout the dialogue with his friends, Job sows the seeds of hope. "O that I might have my request, and that God would grant my desire" (6:8). When faced with the fact of his own mortality, he draws upon an analogy from nature. "For there is hope for a tree, if it is cut down, that it will sprout again, and its shoots will not cease." This leads him to sow the seed of hope for his own future in the form of a question. "If mortals die, will they live again?" His own longing is projected upon God's longing toward him. "You would call and I would answer you; you would long for the work of your hands" (14:7, 14-15).   Even when there is no immediate relief to his suffering, he expresses hope. "But he knows the way that I take; when he has tested me, I shall come out like gold" (23:10). These are not faith statements, but seeds of hope sown in the uprooted and damaged soil of his life.

Before we sow, we need to know the season. I am sowing winter wheat, for it is that season in my life. Not that there has been a failure of faith or lack of a harvest, but it is a time when one realizes that the summer is over. There is a time to grieve the change of seasons. Anticipation of the beginning of one season always entails the end of another. My grand-daughter is to be married in a few months. For her the season is spring. While I meditate on the book of Job to find the will to plant winter wheat, she muses on the Psalm of Solomon. "For now the winter is past, the rain is over and gone. The flowers appear on the earth; the time of singing has come, and the voice of the turtledove is heard in our land" (2:11-12). When she was born I wrote a poem for her that says in part:

> Some part of us (I am told)
> waits to be born in tomorrow's child;
> I dreamed a dream and cast on you the spell
> Of awakening to a life that's both new and old,
> And living with the haunting happy thought
> that you know more than you can ever tell.
> And so, child
> When the familiar eyes in the strange face
> Peers out at you from the gallery
> of grandparents you have known,
> And when you suddenly sense, without being told,
> That part of you is ancient, wise in the
> ways of the spirit;
> And when you reach the promised land,
> And it is yours, to keep and to hold,
> And when you realize that it is a gift,
> And that it is your own life, and it is good,
> then you will know
> > why you have come
> > why you are here
> > and who you are to be;
> Then you will know that it was for this (and for me),
> that you are TONDI

The generations of hope carry us along, pausing now and then, to add some new to the old, to sow their seeds in the soil we have prepared. What others have willed makes us willing to be sowers of a harvest to be reaped, in order to produce seeds yet to be sown. We trust the seed to carry with it the life that we have lived, and in its own life, to become what it longs to be.

Chapter 4 - Germinating

Let the Life of The Seed Do Its Own Work

My first science class was not in the school-room but in my mother's kitchen. In the spring prior to planting time, my father took a dish towel, folded it, spread it on the kitchen table, and carefully laid out 100 kernels of wheat taken from the bin that would supply the sowing for that year's harvest. I was probably only 8 or 9 years old. I watched as he carefully placed ten kernels in ten rows on the cloth, covered with another towel moistened with water, and then placed it carefully on the mantel over the top of the wood-burning stove. "In a few days," he said, "we will look at it and count the kernels that have sprouted in order to determine whether or not we have good seed." As the days passed, I must confess that I occasionally peeked, but did not disturb the seeds, more in fear of my father than of affecting the outcome of the experiment.

When a week had passed, my father took the same carefully folded towels down, placed them on the kitchen table, uncovered the seeds and said, "Good. Looks like most have sprouted." Each seed had produced a small white sprout, except for a very few. Patiently my father picked out each seed that had no sprout and laid it aside. There were only three. "That's a germinating rate of 97%," he said, "good enough for planting." When I asked, "How did you figure that out?" He replied, "Well I placed 100 seeds, and it appears that 97 of them sprouted, that's how you figure percentage."

Later in life I found out that my father had to drop out of school to help with farm work and never completed the 8th grade! I doubt that he attended any science classes, and his math classes probably may have gone so far as to include 'fractions,' but the farm was a pretty good science lab in those days.

The Mystery of the Seed

The fact that seeds contain within themselves a life that only needs a supportive environment to begin to grow is conventional wisdom for those who plant them. This is a mystery that fascinates those who study the genetic structures of organic life but who, despite their scientific knowledge, have no clue as to *why* this should be the way it is. As I wrote earlier (Chapter One), some seeds were discovered at King Herod's palace on Mount Masada, near the Dead Sea that were determined by carbon dating to be over 2,000 years old. When one of these seeds was planted that had been lying dormant since the birth of Jesus, it sprouted and grew a plant. Nothing had to be added except water and a healthy soil environment. Once planted, this 2,000 year old seed did its own work. Within what appeared to a lifeless form, like the kernel of wheat in my father's hand, life sprouted. Scientists may now be able to tell us *how* this is possible, but *why* this should be possible remains a mystery, as does the origin of life itself.

This is not unlike the seed of hope, a longing that emerges from within the human spirit that often can lie dormant, appearing to be dead or, having been silenced by a succession of failed attempts to grow a harvest of hope. Our role is not to create hope, we cannot do that anymore than we can take a bit of rock and make it into a seed. We cannot manufacture hope. But perhaps, as a paramedic might do, we can perform CPR and breathe life into the seed of hope. If hope was implanted in the human spirit as the very 'breath of God' (Gen 2:7), then hope can 'breathe' again as we breathe upon it. Our role is to sow the seed in the soil of our own soul, and tend the seeds planted by others.

In March of 1980, El Salvadorian Archbishop Oscar Romereo, was killed by an assassin's bullet because of his resistance to the brutal tactics of the government against the people. Days before his murder he told a reporter, "You can tell the people that if they succeed in killing me, that I forgive and bless those who do it. Hopefully, they will realize they are wasting their time. A bishop will die, but the church of God, which is the people, will never perish." Before he was killed, he wrote this prayer.

This is what we are about:
We plant the seeds that one day will grow.
We water seeds already planted, knowing that they
    hold future promise.
We lay foundations that will need further development.
We provide yeast that produces effects far beyond our capabilities.
We cannot do everything, and there is a sense of liberation in realizing that.
This enables us to do something, and to do it very well.
It may be incomplete, but it is a beginning, a step along the way,
    an opportunity for God's grace to enter and do the rest.

We may never see the end results, but that is the difference between
     the master builder and the worker.
We are workers, not master builders—ministers, not messiahs.
We are prophets of a future not our own.

This is a more contemporary expression of what the Apostle Paul wrote in
his letter to the Corinthians who were challenging his role as an apostle of
Christ. "I planted, Apollos watered, but God gave the growth. So neither
the one who plants nor the one who waters is anything, but only God
who gave the growth. The one who plants and the one who waters have
a common purpose, and each will receive wages according to the labor
of each" (1 Cor 4:6-8).

The Seed Works by Itself

This is how it is with the seed of hope. It works 'by itself,' as do all
seeds. Our role is not to create hope out of nothing, but to grow hope into
something. In his parable of the Kingdom, Jesus likened the Kingdom to
someone who scattered seed on the ground, "and would sleep and rise
night and day, and the seed would sprout and grow, he does not know
how." But then Jesus added, "The earth produces of itself, first the stalk,
then the head, then the full grain in the head" (Mark 4:26-28). The phrase,
"of itself" is a translation of the Greek word *automatos*, from which we
have our word 'automatic.' The word is used only one other time in the
New Testament, with reference to the time that Peter was arrested and
thrown into prison. When an angel of the Lord came to him and told him
that he was going to be set free, the angel and Peter walked past the first
and second guards and then the gate to the city opened to them "of its
own accord" (automatically).

Is it really that simple? Does the seed of hope 'spring alive' in our
hearts of its own accord? Yes, of course. But, as with the seed that had
been lying dormant for 2,000 years, it must be sown, watered, and tended.
The important thing for us to realize is that hope has its own power of
germination. Thus, even though dormant, it is alive and has the power to
come alive and grow. Could the hope that Archbishop Romereo expressed
in his own martyrdom actually be transmitted to others where it could
germinate and continue to grow? Can the seed of hope be inherited, as
we inherit other physical, mental and even emotional characteristics from
our ancestors?

We are born with longing. And the seed of hope is longing. What is
this natal longing that germinates in our spirit? Is it created anew with
each birth, or are there remnants of longing passed on from generation to
generation? Is this longing without content, or does it already float images

before us that have been fully or partially realized by those from whom we acquire the color of our eyes and even our disposition? It would be unlikely that longing, especially if it moves us toward hope, would be without color and form.

The southern novelist, Thomas Wolfe, caught a glimpse of this long-ing when he wrote, "Which of us has known his brother? Which of us has looked into his father's heart? Which of us has not remained forever prison-pent? Which of us is not forever a stranger and alone? . . . Remem-bering speechlessly we seek the great forgotten language, the lost-lane-end into heaven, a stone, a leaf, an unfound door. Where? When?"

If even the seed of wheat carries within it the color of a former harvest and a reach for the sun while still buried in the soil, should we not be surprised if the seed of hope that arises as a longing in our own soul out of pre-natal sleep already knows the language of hope before it hears the word of hope? We do not need to teach our children how to hope. Hope is germinating in their souls before they learn the word. And if there are languages for which there are no words for hope, there is hope nonethe-less.

Hopelessness is wounded hope, not the absence of hope. Even a hope that is 'wounded unto death,' cannot be extinguished. Even seeds lying dormant for years, if one but provides water and soil, will awaken and begin to live. That which is God-breathed can be wounded but not anni-hilated. As Archbishop Romereo told his people, you can kill a bishop but not the spirit of the body of Christ. The seed of hope not only will survive, it will carry with it a vision of peace that has not yet been accomplished, but which has been sown from the hand of God.

Abraham, we are told, went forth not knowing whither to go except to find a place on earth that would become a threshold from which he could already see a "city that has foundations, whose architect and builder is God" (Heb 11:8-10). The author of Hebrews reminds us that such people as Sarah and Abraham saw the fulfillment of the promise "from a distance" and were "seeking a homeland." That is, to "desire a better country, that is, a heavenly one" (11:14-16). Why would not the 'land of promise' here on earth satisfy this longing? What was germinating within them that led them to dissatisfaction with a land 'flowing with milk and honey' and a hope for a homeland where they had never lived but saw from a distance? It was not as though their lives were some kind of reincarnation of a pre-vious existence, there is no hope in that. But rather the seed of hope, the longing that germinated within them was breathed into them (and us) by the Spirit that walks in the garden of heaven. This is spirit that longs

within us for that 'lost lane-end into heaven.' This is the seed of hope. If
we let it do its work, it will germinate and grow into that living hope of
which Peter wrote: "By his great mercy he has given us a new birth into
a living hope through the resurrection of Jesus Christ from the dead" (1
Peter 1:3). The Spirit of the Christ who has risen from the dead breathes
into our dormant spirits the longing that grows into hope.

Listening to the Voice of Hope

We need to stop sometimes and listen to the voice of that hope rather
than keep stirring the soil after the seed has begun to germinate. Germination takes place in silence, but the growth of hope has its own language,
common to everyone whose ear is turned to the sound. A single kernel of
corn, no larger than a child's fingernail, within 100 days of germination
can produce a green stalk six to eight feet high with at least one ear on it.
In the hot, muggy early summer, when the corn shoot has made its way
above ground, it would grow as much as two or three inches in a single
day. Farmers survived those hot days and nights by saying, "This is good
corn weather!" And, on occasion, when the nights were so still that it
seemed that the stars made music, one would say to another, "It's so still
one can hear the corn growing." Really! I have been there. Perhaps only
those who plant their hope along with the seed in the soil, 'have ears to
hear,' as Jesus once said (Luke 8:8).

The seed of longing has a 'sixth sense' that registers movements whose
sounds are so silent that they are only felt like a sighing of the spirit. I know
those sounds, though I cannot say that I have heard them. The Scripture
tells us that Adam and Eve "heard the sound of the Lord God walking in
the garden at the time of the evening breeze" (Gen 3:8). Isn't that incredible! Each phrase of that sentence is like a chord that lifts us higher and
higher, causes us to pause until the last note fades into the next, and then
deposits us breathless and shaken in a familiar place.

If I heard the sound of the Lord God once in my garden of life, that
would be enough for me. If I heard it I would know it was the Lord. And
even if I could never describe it I would know it. "We can know more than
we can tell," the Scottish philosopher Michael Polanyi once wrote. He
called this a 'tacit knowledge.' Our English 'tacit' comes from the Latin,
tacitus, which has the root meaning of 'silence.' The longing of hope is
carried forward, not by words or actions, but in silence, much like the
germination of any seed. When I 'heard the corn growing' on a warm
summer evening, it was the 'sound of silence.' Not the kind of silence
that was merely an empty chamber waiting to be filled, but a 'pregnant
silence,' as we often say. By which we mean a silence that is filled with

something alive and whose seed is germinating.

There is always the temptation to intrude into that process, either out of curiosity or out of impatience. When I secretly peeked at the sprouting seeds by lifting the cloth cover, I was both impatient and curious, as small boys are wont to be. My Father, being more experienced with the ways of nature, simply waited out the week and then lifted the cloth. He seemed to be able to 'hear' when the kernels sprouted. He had faith in the power of the seed. That is, he 'knew' when it was time by respecting the silence and allowing it to perform the miracle. And it is a miracle, a miracle on which hope rides as a chariot through the spaces between worlds, as small as atomic particles, and large as galaxies. He was not only my first science teacher, but the first one to initiate me into the mystery of faith.

How Faith Protects the Seed of Hope

Let me offer a brief digression to make this point, which I believe contributes to our understanding of how faith allows hope to live in silence.

On Christmas eve the family tradition was to have an oyster stew supper and then go to the church for the annual Christmas program. Herein lies the story. When the last of the stew had been consumed and the last oyster swallowed with relish by my father (with somewhat of a flourish to impress those of us who had not yet acquired the taste), the story began.

"My father used to tell us," my own father would say, "that if you were to go to the barn at midnight on Christmas Eve you would see an amazing sight. At the very stroke of midnight, in honor of the birth of the baby Jesus, all of the cows will stand to their feet. They have an instinct that humans do not have. This knowledge they have inherited from those animals who were in the stable where Jesus was born. It is a wonder to behold!"

Each year as the story was told, my imagination was stimulated. I pictured the cows that I knew so well, each one by name, standing to their feet. I wanted to see this miracle for myself! Each year I would promise myself that just before midnight I would get up and go out to the barn to see this sight. Each year, unfortunately, I would go to sleep and never wake up until morning!

There is a gap in my memory for a few years. I am sure that the story was told, but I do not remember. Then came a year that sealed the story to my heart in a way that will never be forgotten. I was in my early teens, old enough to stay awake and go to the barn and see for myself. As midnight neared, I looked out the window at the barn and thought, "I am finally going to see for myself this miracle."

But I did not go! I remember clearly making the decision not to go and investigate this phenomenon for I realized that I was going out of doubt and not out of faith.

Let me explain. The story told by my father had the power to evoke in my mind an extraordinary thing emerging out of the ordinary. These were ordinary cows, not religious ones! I was caught by the vision of these animals, so well known to me, suddenly standing to their feet in recognition of the birth of Jesus, as a blind and yet compelling act of devotion. It was this vision that stirred my own childlike faith that Jesus was the gift of God and worthy of adoration and worship.

The Scottish Theologian Donald MacKinnon, once put it this way: "Yet the issue of attaching the unfamiliar vision to the familiar description remains; the attachment of the strange to the usual, of the final to the relative." This is precisely what the story did for me. The ordinary and familiar became my connection between the 'strange vision' of the birth of God in a stable in Bethlehem. The story stimulated my imagination and lifted the roof-top of my familiar stable so that my ordinary cows could hear the extraordinary singing of angels!

As a teenager so I thought, I had grown out of this naive childlike faith and wished to prove for myself the things that were believed. In particular, I wanted to see once and for all whether or not the cows would stand up. The key, of course, was the 'whether or not.' It never occurred to me as a young child to question *whether* the cows would stand at midnight, I only wanted to be there when it happened! Likewise, it never occurred to me to question my father as to whether or not he had ever gone to the barn to see this event. Such is the power of a story to compel faith beyond question. Of course my father never had gone to the barn at midnight. For he was not telling me what he had seen but what he had been told and what he could believe based on the one who told it.

There is a certain 'murderous intention' in the need to prove or disprove a story that requires an element of faith to tell and believe. There is a kind of ruthless curiosity which wants to expose a belief as a myth, to be examined like the corpse of an animal one has tracked down and finding it unfit to eat tosses away as worthless.

Somehow, there arose in my heart, looking out the window at the silent barn with the sleeping cows, a whisper of caution. "Once you go," I told myself, "It will never be the same." Some reason beyond reason itself compelled me to pause and consider the consequences. If it were indeed a fact, I could then only tell what I had seen, not what I believe. Faith, the Bible tells us, is "the assurance of things hoped for, the conviction of things not seen" (Hebrews 11:1).

I never did go. I have kept the faith.

For me, the cows still stand at midnight on Christmas eve in honor of the birth of God in a stable. I have a story to tell to my children and grandchildren. What angel it was that whispered in my heart at midnight so many years ago, I may never know. But I will be eternally grateful. My father and I have this in common. We kept the mystery in our hearts and our faith in the story.

I tell this story now in order to point to the relation between faith and hope. Faith guards hope while it sleeps in silence. Faith protects hope from being prematurely forced to display its results and if it cannot, is pounded into bread and not allowed to germinate. The author of Hebrews exhorts us by saying, "Let us hold fast to the confession of our hope" (Heb 10:23).

I can count out the seeds of my hope, I can trace out the longings of my heart, they are precious and precarious. I can hear the sounds of their silent growth in the garden of my life. Or is that the Lord God walking in the evening breeze?

Part Two

SUMMER

The Cultivation of Hope

Brandon
January 5, 1990

Alive!
Torn from the perspiring flesh of others
we scream our pain with fresh-born fears
and reach out blindly for our mothers,
who bind us close with love-torn tears;
 a baptism into life.

Chosen!
Twice wanted means twice blest!
a first birth born with love's consent
to give you life and prepare what's best,
a gifted birth and second advent;
 a baptism into family.

Christened!
In script invisible to all but grace
the water traces out your name;
I write God's image upon your face
and touch your soul with Spirit's flame;
 a baptism into Christ

Storied!
From those who story childhood days
and show the way to heavenly things,
your night is filled with morning rays
and angels touch you with their wings;
 a baptism into faith.

Destined!
The promise given, the trek begun,
the child's last long look toward the earth,
remembers love and becomes a son,
to experience at last another birth;
 a baptism into heaven.

RSA

Chapter 5 - Weeding

If You Didn't Plant it Pluck it

As a small boy on the farm in South Dakota, one of the tasks that I liked least was being sent out to the cornfield on a hot summer day to pull the stalks of sunflowers that were growing amidst the corn. The sunflowers were not planted, they simply grew every year from seeds that were carried over in the soil from one year to another. The sunflower plants were ferocious competitors with the corn. The stalks grew higher than the corn in order that when ripe, the large golden pod filled with seed could have unhindered access to the sun. Beautiful as they were in full bloom, they were considered weeds by my father and if left to grow would deprive the corn of precious water and nutrients from the soil.

What is now quite remarkable, is that in some of the same fields once planted with corn where the sunflowers grew as wild, unwanted weeds, farmers now plant and grow sunflowers in order to sell the seeds for a cash crop! I suppose that somewhere there are small boys sent out into the sunflower fields to pull stalks of corn that grow unwanted and in competition to the sunflowers.

So what is a weed?

Were there weeds in the Garden of Eden or did they emerge after the Fall as some kind of curse on the ground to make the cultivation of the soil more of a burden than it was originally intended to be? Actually, no plant is a weed until it grows amidst a cultivated garden or field. I assume that when Adam and Eve began to cultivate the Garden of Eden before the Fall they intended that some plants flourish and others perish. Adam and Eve were created and given the mandate to 'subdue the earth,' which would involve some kind of cultivation and rule over what otherwise would grow wild. If strawberries were grown for their luscious taste, other plants were plucked from the patch in order that the berries were not deprived of water and nutrients from the soil. Cultivation is cruel to unwanted plants. This is the rule of the garden.

I have often wondered why Adam and Eve, when told not to eat of the tree of the knowledge of good and evil (Gen 2:17) did not simply cut it down. That would have ended that temptation! The problem is, the Scripture also says that the Lord God caused every tree to grow out of the ground, including, "the tree of the knowledge of good and evil" (Gen 2:9). So there goes my solution to the problem. If God planted it they probably ought not to pluck it, just leave it alone!

Can hope be cultivated? Yes, of course. If hope is a seed and can be sown then some attention needs to be given to the growth of hope from that seed. Following the analogy of nature that we are using in this book, the seed of hope does not grow without opposition. There are competing plants in the garden of hope. Some of which were already there and some that emerge through careless self-indulgence and others through what often appears to be a more virulent hostile presence.

In one of Jesus' parables he told of a man who sowed good seed in his field. But while everyone was asleep an enemy came and sowed weeds among the wheat and then went away. So when the plants came up the weeds appeared as well. When the servant reported this to his master he said, "Master did you not sow good seed in your field? Where, then, did these weeds come from? He answered, 'an enemy has done this'" (Mt 13:24-30). In case we should conclude that all 'weeds' are sown in our garden of hope by an 'enemy,' with regard to what defiles us, Jesus said that it does not come from a source outside of us but from within. "It is not what comes from inside that defiles you. For from within, out of a person's heart, come evil thoughts, sexual immorality, theft, murder, adultery, greed, wickedness, deceit, lustful desires, envy, slander, pride, and foolishness. All these vile things come from within; they are what defile you" (Mark 7:20-23 NLT). That is quite a list of weeds!

Are there 'weeds' sown in our garden of hope by the evil one? Yes indeed. Jesus made that quite clear as Peter writes, "Discipline yourselves, keep alert. Like a roaring lion your adversary the devil prowls around, looking for someone to devour" (1 Peter 5:8). When Paul explained why he had not come to the church at Thessalonica he said it was not because of a lack of longing to see them (he hoped!), but "Satan blocked our way" (1 Thess 2:18).

While I allow for the fact that the devil is an adversary and may well at times sow seeds of discord, division and strife in our garden of hope, my concern here is not with the kind of spiritual warfare that challenges the evil one, that is another book. My concern is for the plants that we allow to grow in our own garden of hope because they are all-too familiar to us. These 'weeds' need to be plucked, because we did not sow them in hope, but rather discovered them growing in the same 'seed-bed' with the seed of hope. These are the weeds that do not appear noxious and dangerous, as something sown by an enemy, but as familiar to us as doubt is to a doubter and skepticism to a skeptic. These are temptations, as James reminds us, because they do not come from either God or Satan, "But one is tempted by one's own desire, being lured and enticed by it" (James 1:14). The clue as to the source of these weeds that flourish in our garden of hope and threaten hope itself is that when desire is confused with longing, we are open to deception. This is why James warns, "Do not be deceived, my beloved" (1:16). It would be easier to identify the weeds that threaten hope if they were obviously noxious and defiling due to being immoral. While these kind of weeds need to be rooted out, the weeds that need to plucked out of our garden of hope are more objects of desire rather than enticement to do evil.

We are immediately reminded of the source of temptation in the original Garden of Eden where hope was crushed and despair entered in. The tree of the knowledge of good and evil was not something that enticed them to immoral actions, but rather attracted them to edifying thoughts. "So when the woman saw that the tree was good for food, and that it was a delight to the eyes, and that the tree was desired too make one wise, she took of is fruit and ate; and also gave some to her husband who was with her, and he ate" (Gen 3:6). No wonder they did not cut it down! Who would want to pluck such a plant out of one's own garden? I say again, when longing passes over into desire, the seed of hope is smothered and becomes dormant, its leaves wither, its fruit is never gathered.

Longing is More Than Desire

The confusion of desire with longing makes this discussion difficult. We often use the terms interchangeably. The difference, however, is not a matter of semantics but of substance. I have chosen to use the word longing for the seed of hope rather than desire. Longing includes desire, while desire may not reach as far or go as deep as longing.

The seed of hope is longing. Longing is a desire that goes deeper than mere self-gratification. Longing ignores that which appeals only to our desire in order to bear fruit that fulfills the heart. "Hope deferred makes the heart sick, but a dream fulfilled is a tree of life" (Prov 13:12 NLT). What makes gardening difficult with regard to hope is that we must learn to discern one kind of desire from another. One desire is rooted in the Spirit (what I call longing), the other in what Paul calls the flesh, our natural appetites and instincts for self-gratification. "For what the flesh desires is opposed to the Spirit, and what the Spirit desires is opposed to the flesh; for these are opposed to each other to prevent you from doing what you want" (Gal 5:17). The opposition between flesh and Spirit is exactly the difference between desire and longing.

Weeds are desires that demand immediate and frequent feeding, while longing will go without immediate gratification for the sake of finding deeper fulfillment. Thus longing is a positive value rather than a negative one. When Esau, who was the first-born of the twins, and having a natural claim on the birthright, became famished due to lack of food, he offered to sell his birthright to his brother Jacob. "I am about to die," he said, "of what use is a birthright to me?" (Gen 25:32). He plucked the wrong plant! Immediate desire had taken the place of any longing he might once have had to receive the birthright from his father. This is how we identify the weeds that need to be plucked from our garden of hope.

Earlier, in chapter two, I quoted from a letter that Dietrich Bonhoeffer wrote from prison to his fiancé, Maria, after she had written almost in despair over being separated with little immediate hope of reunion. He wrote, "If our love were merely agonizing deprivation, we should probably die of unassuaged longing in our separate cages. There are already inherent in our love, not deprivation and desire alone, but-miraculously enough--the beginnings of fulfillment. . . Isn't love always, but always, a mutual longing that can never be fully assuaged?" Maria needs to do some gardening. Her need--an immediate solution to their situation in order that her desire to be with him could be satisfied--had come close to smothering the deeper longing that enables love to survive. Indeed, this longing, as he reminded her, was not only some temporary emotion due to their separation, but the very essence of mutual love itself. When love quenches longing in its embrace of immediate satisfaction, hope has already been sacrificed on the altar of desire. And that is a sacrifice that never reaches the level of sacrament.

Longing is sacramental in that it experiences a reality that remains inaccessible to our ordinary senses. It is a 'presence in absence' that brings satisfying peace even as it leaves desire unfulfilled. If hope is viewed as a plant that has been sown by the seed of longing, it has within itself all that is necessary to survive the unfriendly elements if the longing is not weakened by the high-energy demands of other plants in our garden. The life-energy that fuels longing (psychologists might call it ego strength) is self-generating but can easily be diverted within the self by other life-energy demands (ego needs). These demands or ego needs are the plants that need to be recognized and plucked.

The Noxious Weed of Anxiety

Anxiety, for example, is one such weed. Being anxious in the face of uncertainty is quite normal. One can have moments or even short periods of anxiety without depleting the energy of longing. However, when anxiety 'takes root' and becomes more or less a way of life, it becomes a negative discharge of life-energy (ego strength) and is a constant drain on the longing that fuels hope. This is why prolonged periods of anxiety tend to result in feelings of hopelessness. One gets 'stuck' in a pattern where responses to the ambiguity and uncertainty of life create a first response of apprehension and fear, often 'predictive' of negative outcomes.

In the Sermon on the Mount Jesus counsels his disciples not to rely on earthly treasures that are vulnerable to corruption or theft, but to "store up for yourselves treasures in heaven," so that "where your treasure is, here your heart will be also" (Mt 6:19-21). If one tries to serve both God and material wealth one will be deeply divided in the inner self. "Therefore," Jesus says, "I tell you do not worry about your life" (6:25). The Greek word used here means 'anxious, or troubled care' (*merimnao*). To take thought of or care of something or someone is normal. When it becomes 'troubled' care it becomes toxic to the self and to others with a negative effect. Jesus appeals to nature and the birds of the air to make his point. The birds do not sow nor harvest, but are 'taken care of' by the good Creator. As with all parables, one must not press them too far. In this case, Jesus was making the point that the plants of the field and birds of the air live without anxiety in their natural environment. In somewhat the same way, humans can live in a supernatural environment, having immediate needs that relate to their physical/temporal existence but also with 'hope' that goes beyond what their natural life can provide. Nature is unaware of its dependence upon the Creator.

When humans are aware of their dependence upon their Creator they can live with hope that does not cause them to be anxious. If the creatures who live only by their own nature were somehow given hope for life beyond what nature can provide, they would also need to have awareness of their dependence upon the Creator to sustain this hope. Thus hope is linked not with desire or need, which would lead to anxiety, but with the Creator God who has given us this awareness of life beyond the material/temporal world. The gift of this awareness that leads to hope contains within it the spiritual power to sustain hope. But this spiritual power must not become the fuel for 'troubled anxiety.'

If we agree that anxiety of this nature is a noxious plant and needs to be plucked out of our garden of hope, just how do we do that? I can become so anxious about my anxiety that I keep sowing new seeds of anxiety even while trying to pluck out older plants! When Jesus says, in effect, 'just stop being anxious,' he does not give us a prescription that we can take to a psychological pharmacist to be filled as a remedy for anxiety. But let's try it anyway.

Disarming Anxiety

For several years I have team-taught courses with Jeff, who is a Christian psychologist and an effective therapist. His diagnosis for this kind of toxic anxiety is that it stems from a problem of control. Faced with the fact that from the earliest age we are confronted with situations, needs, and choices that often have unknown outcomes, we use control mechanisms to cope with the anxiety produced in us. We ought to be able to control things our mind tells us, and if we can just keep control of things we would not be anxious. The double-bind in this way of thinking, he told me, is that while feeling in control may appear to give us a sense of power over the unknown, it is driven by anxiety so that any threat to our control opens up anxiety again at a deeper level. When faced with the fact that we are not able to control events in our life, anxiety can either turn into panic or depression. Depression can be the way in which the self anesthetizes anxiety; panic can result in irrational behavior. In either case, hopelessness smothers the seed of longing.

But how then does one re-program the self so that the need to control returns to what, in computer language is a default position? Jeff says that the problem is that the need to control is itself a default position manifested by the continued unconscious desire to experience oneself as all-powerful and self-sufficient. He says that the illusion of control is a manifestation of the originally sinful desire to perceive the self as sufficient, in need of no alterations. As such, any attempt to alter or modify the need to control life threatens the self at the core resulting in resistance to change. Kierkegaard once told a parable of the typographical error. If one were to give it self-consciousness and then attempt to correct it, it would protest by saying, "I may be an error in your eyes, but for me it is my very existence." Correction is thus annihilation! This is a plant that does not want to be plucked! If, with one hand, metaphorically speaking, we attempt to uproot it, with the other hand we keep it firmly in place.

The best way to curb anxiety is to stop feeding it. Anxiety is a parasite plant. It has no power source of its own, but lives off the mental and spiritual energy that we provide. It has a taproot that goes right into the core of the self. It emerges in various forms, sometimes concealed as anxious prayer, anxious faith, anxious love and even anxious hope. Maria was anxious; her love was anxious and no doubt her faith was anxious. Dietrich sensed that and wrote: "But this mutual longing mustn't always connote frenzy and insensate desire, it mustn't always afflict and torment us, it needn't be forever fretting over what is still denied us." Without a hint of religiosity or even reference to a biblical text, he encouraged her to reframe her thinking and spoke of the inherent promise of fulfillment (hope) in their love and said, "I constantly cling to that, and my gratitude for it is such that what already exists is far more important to me than what is still to come."

This is virtually a paraphrase of the Apostle Paul who wrote: "Do not worry [be anxious] about anything, but in everything by prayer and supplication with thanksgiving let your requests be known to God. . . Not that I am referring to being in need; for I have learned to be content with whatever I have" (Phil 4:6,11). It is worthy of note that Paul also was in prison when he wrote these words. This man who spent his early life attempting to control his relation with God through zealous keeping of the law, lost control when confronted by Christ. He was blinded, led helpless into the city, and received the fullness of the Holy Spirit when the man he had come to put in chains laid hands on him and prayed (Acts 9:1-19). Paul (Saul) was delivered of anxious hope through the transformation of his mind, where his vital energy was no longer focused on controlling his own life but submitting to the will of God (Rom 12:2).

We forget that submission is not the annihilation of ego-strength so that we remain passive and helpless, but a positive engagement with the reality of the present finding assurance that what we hope for is made certain by the promise of God. We cannot control the future, and very little of the present. Hope is a future reality generated in the present; as such, it is beyond our control but not out of reach. Longing reaches for that which cannot be grasped in the present; this is hope. The certainty of that for which we long can only be granted by the one who controls the future; that is God. Desire seeks to make God a servant in order to give immediate gratification. If one has what one desires there is no need for hope. Failure to receive gratification as an immediate reality leads to hopelessness. Longing avoids both outcomes and keeps hope alive by releasing the self from its dependence upon the immediate in order to gain the eternal. When Jesus said, "Strive first for the Kingdom of God," he was not asking us to become 'weed killers,' that takes a lot of emotional/ spiritual energy (Mt 6:33). Rather he was urging us to become 'kingdom planters.' When we invest in the Kingdom of God for the sake of the renewal of this present life as well as in hope of eternal life, we deprive anxiety of its emotional fuel and it extinguishes itself. Jesus did not have to hunt the demons down and destroy them, he simply banished them, knowing that they have no existence of their own, and would perish by being left to themselves. So it is with the noxious weed of anxiety. You 'pluck it out' of your garden of hope by not feeding and watering it with your own psychical and spiritual energy.

We must always remember that God gives us the spiritual enablement to do what he asks of us in order that we can do what we must do, but cannot do by ourselves. Even Jesus said, "I can do nothing on my own" (John 5:30). What he did was the work of the Father in him, not his own (John 10:37-38). The Apostle Paul says, "For I can do everything through Christ who gives me strength" (Phil 4:13 NLT). John reminded his readers that the Spirit of God that comes to live within us is "greater than the one who is in the world" (1 John 4:4).

I want to take all of my gardening tools with which I weary myself by attempting to keep my garden of hope lush and thriving and hand them over to God, who is my landscape gardener. I yield control, I partner with him. Being a humble servant of the Kingdom is where I invest my energy, and hope. In his marvelous translation of James 1:21, Eugene Peterson renders it thus: "So throw all spoiled virtue and cancerous evil in the garbage. In simple humility, let our gardener, God, landscape you with the Word, making a salvation-garden of your life." *The Message*

<u>Chapter 6 - Watering</u>

Keep it Green if You Want it to Grow

When someone left the farm to go to the city to work my father used to say, "The grass is always greener on the other side of the fence." Later in life, I heard the same saying used when someone left one marriage for another. It is an old proverb. A new twist was given it when I heard a friend who practices marital therapy say, "No, the grass is not greener on the other side of the fence, it is greener where you water it." I am sure that this was not original with him, but instead of merely being descriptive, this new way of saying it was prescriptive. In other words, before you abandon some task or relationship because you think that it is dead or dying, try to keep it growing by giving it some attention.

When one applies this to hope, it makes a lot of sense. If you have planted the seed of hope and watched it germinate, don't give up on it during a dry season. While hope has within itself the power to generate its own growth, it can wither and die of neglect. You need to keep it green if you want it to grow.

Neglect is Passive Euthanasia With Regard to Hope

Hope does not often die through a direct attack. It is more often allowed to die by neglect. A faithful and fruitful gardener knows that lack of water rather than a noxious weed or a leaf-eating bug is likely to kill a plant. Neglect is an insidious enemy of hope because it results from the indifference of the one who has planted the seed of hope toward its growth and maturity. Those who would live with hope need exhortation to keep hope alive.

The Apostle Paul warns his spiritual son, Timothy, "Do not neglect the spiritual gift you received through the prophesy spoken over you when the elders of the church laid their hands on you" (1 Tim 4:14 NLT). In his second letter to Timothy, Paul reiterated his exhortation not to neglect what had been given him. "For this reason I remind you to rekindle the gift of God that is within you through the laying on of my hands" (2 Tim 1:6). While the metaphor of 'rekindling' has more to do with fanning a spark of fire than watering, the point is the same. While Paul does not identify the spiritual gift, and hope is not mentioned in the list of spiritual gifts (Rom 12; 1 Cor 12; Eph 4), we would not be wrong in applying this exhortation to hope as well. The author of the book of Hebrews exhorts us: "Let us hold fast to the confession of our hope without wavering, for he who has promised is faithful" (Heb 10:23).

But why do we have to be encouraged and exhorted to 'water' hope, to give it the attention needed to keep it alive? If neglect is so obvious when it has finally destroyed hope, like a garden left un-watered during a hot summer, how does it happen that the very one who has sown the seed of hope should be the one to allow it to die through neglect? The signs of neglect are clear and compelling, except to the one who is neglectful. Neglect is not a conscious decision to deprive hope of the 'water' that nourishes it. Rather by its very nature, neglect is oblivious to its own fault. For this reason, a faithful and fruitful gardener is not an expert in measuring the levels of neglect, but in the shades of green. One does not need to study neglect. It is not in the horticulture curriculum of growing a healthy garden.

In many years of marriage counseling while a pastor I discovered that neglect was the complaint most often voiced by one of the marriage partners. The one accused of being neglectful was usually surprised and defensive. Neglect is a habit, and habits are hard to break. In pre-marital counseling I often tried to point out how neglect can become a habit. Prior to living together persons who create and nourish relationships do so intentionally. This involves planning, communication and coordination in order that a 'meeting' takes place. As the relationship moves toward a more permanent commitment with shared hope of a married life together, this hope is kept alive through the 'meetings' that take place, not by accident, but through creative purpose, often deliberately intended to raise expectations in the other person.

The fact that marriage makes relationship so convenient, I explain, can actually result in the couple losing hope because mutuality can replace mutual longing, as Bonhoeffer reminded his finacé, Maria. Loss of mutual longing can result in mutual neglect. Longing for another is usually experienced as hoping to meet with the other in order that love can create moments of reality that otherwise would not exist. To experience such moments is what love hopes for. If one or the other should neglect to be present at the meeting, longing is betrayed by indifference, and hope begins to wither and die. If this should happen with regularity prior to marriage, the relationship itself cannot survive, except that one becomes the enabler of the other and marriage itself becomes the object of longing, rather than the other person. This is a marriage that begins without hope.

Assuming that a healthy relationship exists prior to marriage, and that hope is alive and well, two things happen rather quickly to cause neglect. The first is convenience and the second is conventionality. Convenience becomes a habit of mutual togetherness that does not require a 'meeting.' Remember, a meeting is something that would not take place until each is present to the other with expectation and openness to the gift of the other. When a married couple settle into the routine of everyday life, their times of being together are more often than not the result of work schedules and daily routine. No 'meetings' have to be arranged, they just happen regularly, it is so convenient to be married! However, convenience is an empty watering can in the garden of hope. When the plant dies, the response is, "Oh, I thought you were doing the watering as I always saw the watering can in the garden!" It is so convenient to have someone else do the watering. Because life is often precarious and unpredictable in so many ways, we crave the security of habit rather than risk creating new meetings where the eyes of the other may not always hold the expectancy we desire nor gaze back into ours with the response we seek.

The second layer of neglect arises through conventionality. The roles of husband and wife are ordinarily not created out of love but put on as wedding garments that have 'permanent press' on the labels. Culture, if not our immediate family, no longer want to think of us as lovers but as husband and wife and, sooner or later, as mother and father. How many wives have not heard the words from their mothers, "I was so hoping to be a grandmother, what are you waiting for?" Love is unconventional and inconvenient. That is why it is called love. And that is why love dies more often out of habit than by hostility. Hostility usually is the emotional response to neglect on the part of a marriage partner. In the blaze of hostility one looks for the smoldering ember of neglect. When hope has died, it may be that neglect has already turned its back. The revival of hope is often beyond the technique of the most experienced marital therapist. Hope can come alive, that is true, but that is a moment of emotional awareness that can only be created by spiritual repentance, for neglect is a spiritual deficit in a relationship not merely an emotional habit.

In preparing a couple for marriage I explain, best as I can to romantic idealists, that 'meeting' is the renewable energy of mating. Finding one's life-time mate is one goal of adulthood. This often happens through a series of 'meetings' that are not convenient and not always conventional. Having one's mate in the house is so convenient that meetings may never happen, and I am not talking about a crisis-driven meeting over budget or time schedules. And even less am I talking about a physical (sexual) meeting where habit may conceal the kind of neglect that drains the energy of longing of all hope. Mating without meeting is not making love.

I often remind couples who are about to marry that their marital relation depends upon their relation as friends, not on their roles as husband and wife. Often married couples say and do things to each other that would destroy a friendship. Because we value the person with whom we are friends, we anticipate the **effect** of our words and actions and hold in check that which would be hurtful and offensive. If we did not, we would soon have no friends. If married persons valued each other as friends, care would be taken not to violate the relation through words and actions which hurt. In the same way, members of the body of Christ are to value each other and take care for the effect of their words and actions upon one another.

It is for this reason that I have written the marriage vows so as to include the promise of meeting as well as mating.

> I pledge my love to you,
> I will cherish and honor you,
> I promise to be open and honest to you,
> to be your friend and companion in life,
> to stand by and support you,
> in happiness as well as in hardship;
> I want always to be coming to meet you,
> and to create a place for our love.

The inclusion of the promise to be a friend is more creative and powerful than the promise to be a husband or a wife. Friendship is the only human bond that exists solely because it is maintained by mutual interest, trust and communication. More than any other human relationship, friendship may come the closest to touching the image and likeness of God in human form. When Paul speaks of the relation of Christ to the church, he appeals to the 'one flesh' relation of human sexuality as a paradigm (Ephesians 5:31-32). That may well be. But Paul, who gives no evidence of having a wife, and Jesus, who never married, both see friendship as expressing the essence of spiritual communion. In his famous 'hymn of love' (1 Cor 13), Paul sings of a love that empowers friendship as surely as that of marriage. While marriage is a metaphor of Christ's relation to the church as his bride, friendship passes beyond the language of metaphor to speak of the essential bond of spirit to spirit.

Beyond our need for intimacy as a fulfillment of love's desire, is the balancing value of companionship with mutual faith in a shared destiny. Beyond our longing for self-fulfillment as a hunger for recognition and happiness in life is the spiritual joy of friendship as the boundary of God's presence--"Where two or three are gathered in my name, I am there among you" (Mt 18:20).

But we are talking here about hope that goes beyond human relationships. If hope can be destroyed through neglect between humans, how much more is hope vulnerable to neglect with respect to our relationship to God. Here too, we need to 'keep it green in order to keep it growing.'

Keeping Hope Alive

James Houston encourages us to view prayer as an essential aspect of a relationship with God and as such, one of the most important ways of keeping hope alive. "Prayerfulness is the breath of relationship, an antidote to the godless poison of secular psychoanalysis. Prayer becomes intertwined with the desire to be indwelt by the Holy Spirit as we relate to others. It has a strong social character and purpose, expressed in supplication and intercession on behalf of others, and also a private purpose, contributing to our own spiritual formation. Indeed, I have found it impossible to separate prayer from friendship."

Ah, there is that word again—friendship! Jesus spoke of friendship with his disciples and suggested that their relation to him should not be construed as merely a servant to a master, but friend to friend. "I do not call you servants any longer, because the servant does not know what the master is doing; but I have called you friends, because I have made known to you everything that I have heard from my Father" (John 15:15). He drew them beyond partnership into intimacy, and beyond intimacy into friendship. He did this through sharing with them his own mission and making them companions of his own life-journey.

With friends, conversation is a form of prayer for it involves communion rather than mere communication. When relationships are primarily based on communication, even when striving to be effective, there are sure to be misunderstandings, even feelings of annoyance. Even Jesus had a lot of trouble communicating with his disciples at times. They often misconstrued what he was saying. "This teaching is difficult; who can accept it?" Jesus replied, "It is the Spirit that gives life . . . The words that I have spoken to you are spirit and life" (John 6:60, 63). Communion is itself an event of spirit, both with regard to humans and with God. Hope thrives on communion.

I begged for a lot for things from my parents. There is a kind of prayer that views God as a parent who only gives us what we beg for. There is some truth to that. God is our Father and through Jesus his Son, we are encouraged to make our requests known to him. But this is not the kind of prayer that keeps hope alive. Too often, when we attach our hope to what we beg for, our hopes are shattered when we do not receive what we want.

With friends, it is entirely different. I do not beg from a friend, though I am free to share my needs and concerns. This kind of prayer is often spontaneous and 'friendly.' It is the kind of prayer that may be intended when the Apostle Paul exhorts us to "pray without ceasing" (1 Thess 5:17). I never cease to be in relationship with a friend even though we are not always having a conversation. Prayer keeps hope alive because it maintains an open connection with God as opposed to what we call in computer language, a 'dial-up' connection with the internet. When my computer is connected to the internet through a special line I can immediately access what I am looking for without having to establish a new connection each time. Isn't that a nice analogy of having a 'prayer-line' open at all times?

Dietrich Bonhoeffer urged his students to pray as a means of experiencing the reality of God and as an antidote to what I have called neglect. "Prayer is the supreme instance of the hidden character of the Christian life. It is the antithesis of self-display. When people pray, they have ceased to know themselves, and know only God whom they call upon. Prayer does not aim at any direct effect on the world; it is addressed to God alone, and is therefore the perfect example of undemonstrative action."

Paul always speaks of prayer when writing to the churches that God created through his ministry. The prayer for the church at Colossae is one such prayer. "In our prayers for you we always thank God the Father of our Lord Jesus Christ, for we have heard of your faith in Christ Jesus and of the love that you have for all the saints, because of the hope laid up for you in heaven. You have heard of this hope before in the word of the truth, the gospel that has come to you. Just as it is bearing fruit and growing in the whole world, so it has been bearing fruit among yourselves from the day you heard it and truly comprehend the grace of God" (Col 1:36). Paul did not plant the church and then leave it to others to do the watering. Through prayer he continued to nourish the hope that he shared with them through the gospel.

Experienced gardeners know that some plants grow better next to others; hope is like that. The author of the book of Hebrews reminds us of this truth: "Let us think of ways to motivate one another to acts of love and good works And let us not neglect our meeting together, as some people do, but encourage one another, especially now that the day of his return is drawing near" (Heb 10:24-25 NLT).

"I know only enough of God to want to worship him, by any means ready to hand," wrote Annie Dillard.

Along with prayer, participating in a worshipping, loving community is a vital aspect of keeping hope alive. We are exhorted not to neglect to meet together "as some people do." One can only wonder what happens to those who do neglect to participate in the body of Christ as an active member. Some have become discouraged and disillusioned with the church and say: "Jesus yes; the church no." But this is not possible. While it is true that some forms of the institutional church may have 'neglected' the gospel and have only the form of Christ's community but not the reality, the concept of a solitary Christian is unknown in the Bible. Even in prison, Paul keeps others close by and in one of his last letters, laments the loss of some from his inner circle of friends and asks that Timothy come and bring Mark with him (2 Tim 4:9-13).

Our hope is 'in Christ.' Not that we use Christ as one would use a stock certificate to provide collateral for a loan. To hope in Christ is to be in Christ. We do not possess Christ as an individual, but we experience Christ through participation in his body, the Christian community.

"Christ exists as community," wrote Dietrich Bonhoeffer in his writing on the nature of the church. *"The personal unity of the church [Kirche] is 'Christ existing as church-community [Gemeinde]; Paul could also speak of Christ himself being the church. Being in Christ means being in the church."* Participation in Christ is participation in his body. Not to belong to the body, says Paul, is to be deprived of the mutual gifts of the Spirit that are given for edification as well as ministry (1 Cor 12). The church that emerges with each generation is the body of Christ comprised of persons who have received the 'birth gift' of the Spirit. These are the members of Christ's body who are joined in a community of love by the "one Spirit, one hope, one Lord, one faith and one baptism" of which Paul wrote (Eph. 4:4-5). The 'one hope' is attached to those who have been baptized by the Spirit into the one body (1 Cor 12:12-13). Hope is thus a mutual life in the body of Christ rather than an individual possession.

While living in Scotland I read the story of a Scottish minister of a small church in the highlands. One of his parishioners had dropped out of the church. The minister went to call on him. Sitting with him quietly in front of the coal-burning fireplace, the minister finally took a set of tongs and selected one burning coal from the pile of coals and set it aside by itself on the hearth. The two sat in silence watching the bright red coal slowly turn to black and then lose its fire completely. The man finally turned to the minister and said, "Pastor, I will be back with the church this week."

John Macmurray says it well: "I need you to be myself. This need is for a fully positive personal relation in which, because we trust one another, we can think and feel and act together. Only in such a relation can we really be ourselves. If we quarrel, each of us withdraws from the other into himself, and the trust is replaced by fear. We can no longer be ourselves in relation to one another." Macmurray goes on to say that when we are in conflict with one another only reconciliation which restores the original confidence and trust can overcome the negative motivation which results in hostility. Apart from this kind of reconciliation we remain isolated individuals. "What we really need," he suggests, "is to care for one another, and we are only caring for ourselves. We have achieved society, but not community. We have become associates, but not friends." The achievement of community of persons is grounded in actions which embody intentionality to "share a common 'soul' or a common history and a common destiny. Macmurray adds: 'The inherent ideal of the personal is a community of persons in which each cares for all the others, and no one cares for himself."

The wisdom of the Preacher in the book of Ecclesiastes puts it plainly. "Two are better than one, because they have a good reward for their toil. For if they fall, one will lift up the other; but woe to one who is alone and falls, and does not have another to help" (Ecc 4:8-10).

Recent publication of Mother Theresa's private journal reveals that she experienced times of deep spiritual depression, lack of faith and virtual hopelessness. All of this despite the fact that she is a modern icon of Christian ministry to the poor and by all accounts, on the 'fast track' to becoming a saint in the Roman Catholic Church. This revelation has caused a great deal of consternation among other believers and some self-satisfied confirmation to the atheists, who seized upon this news as proof that belief in God was a hoax all along. Both have missed the point. Hope is not the private virtue of a saint but the vibrant life of a community (of saints) by the Apostle Paul's definition (1 Cor 1:2). Not to worry, sister Theresa, we will keep your hope alive. There are many gardeners in the garden of hope.

Chapter 7 - Pruning

Not Every Branch is Meant to Bear Fruit

I am thankful that I raised field crops when I farmed and did not have to tend a garden or an orchard. Wheat and corn did not require any pruning. Once the seed was sown, other than cultivating and spraying for weeds, I left the plants to grow in whatever way they wanted. I am well aware that grape vines must be pruned, rose bushes must be cut back, and trees need to be trimmed. I not only do not have the skill necessary to do this kind of work, there is something about cutting off a perfectly good branch in order to give others a better chance that seems unnatural! On the other hand, the original Garden of Eden apparently needed some pruning as well. God placed Adam and Even in the garden to "till it and keep it" (Gen 2:15). I assume that to 'keep' a garden one must prune it, otherwise, if left to grow wild it is probably by definition not a garden.

Having said that, I recognize the value of the metaphor of pruning when it comes to sowing and growing the seed of hope. Only once in the New Testament is the word pruning used as a metaphor drawn from nature as applied to one's spiritual life and growth. In his well-known section on the vine and the branches (John 15), Jesus calls himself the vine and his Father the vinegrower. "Every branch that bears fruit he prunes to make it bear more fruit" (John 15:2). If Jesus is the vine, and we are the branches, as he went on to suggest, then we are not the one doing the pruning but rather might well be the 'pruned' branches! While that is a warning that we should take to heart, this is not the direction I wish to go with regard to the metaphor. My point in citing this passage is to suggest that with regard to the garden of hope that each of us sows and tends, there may well be need of pruning, else what was intended to be a garden becomes more like a jungle.

I do understand this much about pruning. The few trees around our house tend to grow steadily as the growing season is year-round and there is ample water. I have to be reminded that they need pruning. They always look fine to me, they look just like trees are supposed to look. But I am no longer living on a farm where trees are as much a windbreak when growing alongside a field as they are specimens to be admired for the care given to them. So I dutifully summon a 'tree man' to come and prune the tress. Again, it is not just that I no longer like (or should) be climbing around in a tree, but I would not know what branches to lop off and which should remain. For the same reason, I am never asked to prune the rose bushes, though no ladder is required.

The only other passage in the New Testament that seems to suggest something like pruning is the exhortation to accept the discipline of the Lord, though at times it may seem harsh and unfriendly. "My child do not regard lightly the discipline of the Lord, or lose heart when you are punished by him; for the Lord disciplines those whom he loves, and chastises very child whom he accepts" (Heb 12:5-6). The author does recognize that such discipline may not be well received when adminis- tered. "Now discipline always seems painful rather than pleasant at the time, but later it yields the fruit of righteousness to those who have been trained by it" (Heb 12:11).

But if I am to make use of this metaphor for the purpose of this book, I need to take the 'pruning hook' firmly in hand and suggest why and in what ways it is needed for the cultivation of hope. Rather than assuming that it is God who does the pruning, as the scriptures cited above suggest, I am going to put a twist on the concept by assuming that we are the ones who need to do some pruning, especially with regard to hope.

I begin by acknowledging certain principles drawn from those who have mastered the art of pruning as guidelines. Pruning, as with any other skill, requires knowing what you are doing to achieve success. And success with regard to hope means that hope maintains a healthy growth toward maturity, that is bearing good fruit. The old idea that anyone with a chain saw or a pruning saw can be a landscape pruner is far from the truth. More trees may be killed or ruined each year from improper pruning than by pests. Pruning is the removal or reduction of certain plant parts that are not required, that are no longer effective, or that are of no use to the plant. It is done to supply additional energy for the development of flowers, fruits, and limbs that remain on the plant. Pruning, which has several definitions, essentially involves removing plant parts to improve the health, landscape effect, or value of the plant. Once the objectives are determined and a few basic principles understood, pruning primarily is a matter of common sense.

Good. Common sense may give us some guidance when it comes to applying this metaphor to the cultivation of hope. For example, recent news reports with regard to the effect of hurricanes tell of many trees that were blown over, some causing damage to homes and automobiles because they were overgrown. In some cases, the trees remained standing while large limbs were blown off causing the damage. In other cases, the trees had simply grown too large to be sustained by the root system and were destroyed. If some of these trees had been properly trimmed, we were told, the damage would not have been so severe.

Scaling Hope Down to Size

If you ask people if they have too much hope, most will say that they do not have enough. Most will say that they need to increase the size and scope of their hope. If they could just increase hope so that it loomed larger in their life, many people would see that as good. The fact is, the larger and more overblown our hope is the more vulnerable it is when under attack, and hope is always an easy target for the enemy. I have already alluded to the analogy of the windstorm. An overgrown untrimmed tree will often be the first one to fall. So it is with hope. When we keep increasing the size of our hope, much like additions to our house, the more difficult it is to support it when the opposition comes.

This can be somewhat like the prosperous farmer in Jesus' parable; he kept planting large crops, harvesting more grain, until he had more than even he had hoped for and said to himself, "I will do this; I will tear down my barns and build larger ones, and there I will store all my grain and goods. And I will say to my soul, Soul, you have ample goods, laid up for many years; relax, eat, drink, and be merry." But, as Jesus told the story, God said to him, "You fool! This very night your life is being demanded of you. And the things you have prepared, whose shall they be" (Luke 12:16-21)? We are only fooling ourselves when we attach hope to possessions. Hope is strongest when it is least dependent upon the results of our own efforts. Here is where pruning enters in. Too many possessions are like a tree with overgrown branches, they will be the first to fall.

Let me offer a different analogy. A sailing ship is moved by the wind. The larger the sail the more wind it will catch and the faster it will move through the water. But any experienced sailor, when the wind rises to gale force will trim the sails. To sail into the face of a storm with all sails up is inviting a shipwreck. Hope is like that. We raise the sail of hope in order to catch a favorable wind to move us closer to our objective. The larger the sail the more ambitious the hope; this gives us the feeling that we are gaining momentum in life. But when hope is like a ship with untrimmed sails it is in greater peril than a ship with no sail at all.

When we apply the metaphor of pruning to hope, it is a matter of scaling hope down to size. We tend to place our hope in too many things. Rather than hope having a single objective as an expression of a longing of the spirit for that which only God can fulfill, we often are tempted to let our desires create new branches of hope. We cannot invest our hope in everything that we desire.

When desire leads to hope, then what we hope for is little more than what we wish for. As a small boy, when bored I was prone to say, "I wish I had that," or, "I wish I could do that." My mother would respond out of her Danish trove of proverbs: "If wishes were horses all beggars would ride." The reason I remember it so well is probably because it made no sense to me at the time and only frustrated me all the more. When wishes become hopes, we have spread our emotional and spiritual investments too widely and not wisely. When hope becomes attached to desire rather than to longing, it tends to flourish like new branches growing out of the vine. But it is the vine, not the branches that carries the burden of hope. And hope must be able to bear the burden of broken dreams, unfulfilled promises, and delayed gratification. Better to prune off these branches than have them torn off, leaving the vine itself bruised and wounded.

When our hope extends in every direction it is childish and immature. It is short-term and short-lived. It flickers brightly for an instant and then just as quickly dissolves with the first tears of frustration over the loss of some simple pleasure. Hope that can be washed away with the first summer storm is merely a fantasy of the mind, an illusion which shares the same bed with fear--both are ghosts in the night and cannot survive the bright light of day.

Hope requires risk, so much that it hurts. Here is where pruning has its purpose. Better to trim off unfruitful branches before they break off. Hope makes us vulnerable to future and even greater loss. Hope exposes us to disappointment, frustration and betrayal. Faith plants the seed and promises a harvest, and so creates hope. But with the promise of a harvest comes the possibility that the promise will fail. That is the betrayal that hope must bear. Without faith as the investment of one's precious life and resources in the power of life, the burden of hope could not be borne. But faith bears that burden in partnership with hope, for it is partnership with God, the author and creator of life.

The burden of hope bears the responsibility for taking up life again when there has been foolishness and failure. The story of the prodigal son is not the story of one who came home and negotiated a better deal, but of the restoration of a son who had squandered his inheritance (Luke

15). To be a servant is a daily burden. To be a son is a lifetime task, with the risk of failure assumed once more. Only a son can become a prodigal. He did not dare hope for so much, but when he was restored along with the restoration came a new kind of hope, one that had been trimmed of fantasy and foolishness, scaled to size in order to gain the inheritance.

The Apostle Paul uses another metaphor to make the same point. He thinks of himself as an athlete who is running a race. "All athletes are disciplined in their training. They do it to win a prize that will fade away, but we do it for an eternal prize. So I run with purpose in every step. . . I discipline my body like an athlete, training to do what it should. Otherwise, I fear that after preaching to others I myself might be disqualified" (1 Cor. 9: 25-27 NLT). The author of the book of Hebrews has the same metaphor in mind, "Let us strip off every weight that slows us down, especially the sin that so easily trips us up. And let us run with endurance the race that God has set before us" (Heb 12:1 NLT).

We often speak of tough love when we want to urge someone to exercise discipline rather than permissiveness when parenting a young adult child who is living a self-indulgent and potentially disastrous life. This is love with a pruning knife. But we might also speak of 'tough hope' to make somewhat the same point. In this case, we are both the one with the pruning knife and the vine that needs pruning. We need to take an inventory of our hope much like we might do with a stock portfolio. Are we making a lot of bad investments? Are some of our hope investments high maintenance with low dividends? I am willing to pay the college tuition for my daughter, but that is an investment in her future not my own. I take that investment out of my hope portfolio and put it in the one marked 'current obligations' along with my automobile lease contract. When my hope is tied to some one else's success, I not only make that person a slave to my need for self-gratification but become a controlling kind of person, driven by the kind of 'anxious care' against which Jesus warned.

Tough hope needs to be 'lean and mean,' to use a vernacular expression, in order to avoid getting too much wind in its sail or too many branches to support. After all, hope is about a harvest. Unproductive limbs need to be lopped off. Hope that does not produce is not only a poor investment but a devastating blow to the human spirit.

Making Hope More Productive For You

The fact that hope should have immediate benefits to the self was hinted at by Bonhoeffer's prison letter to Maria (cited in Chapter Two). "There are already inherent in our love, not deprivation and desire alone, but--miraculously enough--the beginnings of fulfillment. I constantly cling to that, and my gratitude for it is such that what already exists is far more important to me than what is still to come."

I hardly know how to comment on that!

Just as I am writing this, a letter came from one of my students who has been serving time in the California Institute for Women for the past 28 years. She has taken courses from me in theology through the Distance Learning Program at our seminary. Linda Lee was in the house when her live-in boyfriend killed her two year-old daughter while her older daughter was also in the home. Because she was viewed by the court as an accomplice, she was sentenced to 15 years to life. During her incarceration she became a vibrant Christian woman, completed a college degree by extension, and has earned a certificate in Ministry from our Seminary. She ministers hope and faith on a daily basis to other inmates. For the past 8 years the parole board has recommend unanimously that she be released on parole. Each year the Governor has turned down the board's recommendation. Members of my church have prayed for her release and written many letters on her behalf. Just two weeks ago she was told that the Governor has once again turned down the recommendation for parole. This, despite assurance from the parole board that this time they 'would make it stick' with the Governor.

In the letter that I just opened, Linda expressed her disappointment but wrote: "The greatest lesson I have learned these last months is about living with hopefulness. I had long loved, and yet had issues with Rom 5:3-5. God promises us that 'hope maketh not ashamed,' and yet it is very embarrassing to explain that God has denied me my freedom again when so many have been hoping and praying for me. But I've finally found the concept that clarified this for me. I have too often confused the OBJECT of my hope (the parole) with the SUBJECT of my hope—Christ Jesus. Instead of hoping 'for,' I must hope 'in.' I will not always get what I hope for, but I will never be disappointed by hoping in Christ."

She is a branch that bears fruit. This is the vine of which Jesus spoke.

My student (my teacher!) reminds us that while hope must have its center in that which lies beyond the self, its power must be realized and felt in the heart. She has experienced the productive power of hope. For hope to be productive in our lives it must also be resident in the feeling self, not merely held in the mind as an abstract concept. If hope is to be a 'steadfast anchor of the soul,' as the author of Hebrews put it, it must be experienced in the self along with faith. For hope to have spiritual power it must be more than a statement of what one believes. It must be a productive hope, not merely a future hope. But how does hope produce a benefit in the present when it appears to be oriented to the future?

In her letter Linda went on to write, "By living in hope that God will make all these struggles and disappointments worthwhile in the accomplishing of His purposes, I have been able to refute bitterness. This is God's great miracle and consolation. Life is not avoiding struggle; it is about living well through the struggle."

Linda has pruned the branches of bitterness through the productive power of hope. Bitterness, like anxiety, is a noxious weed that cannot live except we feed it. She did not 'feed' the noxious weed of bitterness, but 'pruned' it by feeding her sisters in prison. The next day after receiving the word that her parole had been denied, she "cooked a Mexican Fiesta for 18 in 100 degree heat. I had promised my friends either a 'farewell' or an 'oh well' party, and sharing comfort food is a good way to connect with people and strengthen bonds."

The spiritual work of pruning is not one that requires a weapon. We are not called by the Spirit to 'hack away' at the branches of bitterness but rather to 'nourish' the hope that lies within us as the very life of Christ, who is the vine (John 15). The *content* of hope is not *what* we hope for, but *who* is our hope, that is Christ. And the Spirit of Christ is the present reality of Christ filling and flooding our own inner life with *hope*. When Christ becomes the experienced content of our longing, hope produces inward peace. Peace is not the absence of struggle or even disappointment, it is not a vacuum, but a positive presence. When Jesus promised that the Holy Spirit would come to be with his disciples after he left, he described this, not as a religious experience but as one that brought peace and freedom from fear and anxiety. "My peace I give to you" (John 14:27). The peace of Jesus through the indwelling of the Holy Spirit does not 'arm' us with a weapon but 'fills' us with his presence.

"I can do all things through him who strengthens me," Paul wrote from prison (Phil 4:13). I do not think that he waited until he was put in prison to do the pruning. Nor should we. Pruning is best done during the growing season. And part of pruning is to nourish our own souls and starve the noxious weeds.

Chapter 8 -Waiting

Patience is the Creative Work of Hope

A dry-land farmer in Texas was asked how his crops were doing? "Don't know," he replied, "haven't looked at them since planting. Can't do anything about it anyway. Will go out at harvest to see what's there." While his display of patience was extraordinary, it cannot be applied to a gardener. As I have written in the preceding chapters, watering and pruning require some visits and some special attention. Even so having been a dry-land farmer in South Dakota where the harvest depended more upon the rainfall and weather than my personal observation, I must confess that I made more than one trip to the field just to see 'how the crops were doing.' Not having access to an irrigation system, there really wasn't anything I could do about lack of water. I had to trust 'mother nature' to attend my crops; but if my impatience betrayed lack of trust, 'she' did not seem to notice. After all, my impatience was mild, more a matter of curiosity and sleepless nights than any desire to take matters into my own hand. The German philosopher, Frederick Nietzsche, once opined, "The pine tree seems to listen, the fir tree seems to wait, and neither with impatience: they give no thought to the little people below them whose impatience and curiosity eat them up alive." Impatience seems to be a common trait in humans. Learning patience is one way of measuring growth toward maturity.

The Anatomy of Impatience

In matters pertaining to hope, impatience may not be so benign. Consider the situation with Abraham and Sarah. After Abraham complained to God that he lacked an heir, he was promised a son. Abraham believed the Lord, "and the Lord reckoned it to him as righteousness" (Gen 15:1-6). However, as it happened, his wife Sarah, was barren and could not bear children. When ten years had passed (Gen 16:3), and Sarah had still not conceived, Sarah gave her servant maid Hagar to her husband, and a son was born, whose name was Ishmael (Gen 16). Thirteen years after the original promise, when Abraham was now ninety-nine years old, God again appeared to him and reiterated the promise and made it even more specific by saying that he would bless the barren womb of Sarah and that she would bear the promised son. Abraham was astonished and told the Lord that he already had a son, who was now thirteen years old. "Oh that Ishmael might live in your sight," cried Abraham (Gen 17:18). But the answer was no. For all that Abraham had invested in Ishmael as the child of hope, it had to be disinvested. He was only the child born of impatience.

Am I wrong in attributing some degree of impatience to Abraham and Sarah resulting in the birth of Ishmael? It would seem only natural from a human perspective. But what then are we to make of Ishmael? While God did make some provision for Ishmael, this was more of a concession to Abraham than part of God's purpose. One can only speculate as to the difference it would have made in the lives of Abraham and Sarah, not to mention Isaac, if Ishmael had never been born. The sibling rivalry and hostility between the two sons and their descendants are still continuing. On the other hand, the blessing of Ishmael, even though he was conceived and birthed due to impatience, indicated that Ishmael also was to be included in the covenant promise given through Isaac. Ishmael and his descendants could have a share in the covenant provided that the sibling relationship remained intact. The seed of impatience is not automatically excluded from God's promise. But when Ishmael set himself against his brother and attempted to claim on his own part the covenant blessing, hostility and even violence resulted.

History is a narrative of the struggle between impatience and patience. Our lives have their own narratives. We have, metaphorically speaking, children of impatience. These are consequences of impulsive, even desperate actions by which we seek fulfillment and bargain with our destiny in order to move hope closer to our grasp. But as with Ishmael, though conceived of impatience, he was ultimately blessed, an encouragement to us that what results from impatience can be redeemed. The grace of God extends hope even to the children of impatience.

There are degrees of impatience, of course. I am not speaking of the kind of impatience that is merely irritating or frustrating--getting caught in traffic when we are late for an appointment, choosing the wrong checkout line at the market. I am thinking of the kind of impatience that creeps in when we have sown and are tending the seed of hope. Remember that the seed of hope is a deep longing for that which can only be realized through God's promise and in God's time. This kind of hope requires trusting and waiting, especially when barrenness and adversity threaten the conception and completion of what is claimed by promise.

This is the kind of impatience that Dietrich Bonhoeffer recognized in the letters sent to him in prison by his fiancé, Maria. In his response, from which I quoted in Chapter Two, he wrote back to her: "But this mutual longing mustn't always connote frenzy and insensate desire, it mustn't always afflict and torment us, it needn't be forever fretting over what is still denied us." There was nothing that she could do to overcome the circumstances that separated them and which denied her what she longed for. There was no Ishmael to comfort her, her impatience had become a 'frenzy' of anxiety. Longing had become a sickness, hope a vacuum of despair.

There is a footnote to the story, from Dietrich's side at least. He had become friends with the guard who helped smuggle in and out books and correspondence. When it appeared that there was no legal means by which Dietrich could be released, and when the circumstances surrounding Hitler's suspicion of those involved in the conspiracy grew deadly, the guard arranged for Dietrich to escape, even providing a change of clothes. Both the guard and Dietrich were to escape and find refuge with friends, safe from Hitler's Gestapo. But at the last minute, when Dietrich realized that his escape would cause retaliation against his family members, he refused to go. Was this his Ishmael that never came to birth? Or was it a miraculous provision that would confirm that he was Isaac? Such is the dilemma of living (and dying) by holding to hope secured by the bond of love. Would he and Maria have finally found refuge and realized their life together for which they both longed? Or would impatience create its own child of history alongside of the promise? Even in retrospect, it is difficult to say. But we know that for Maria, the decision would have been quite different due to the depth of her desire; her patience had come to and end. His had moved to greater maturity.

In an earlier meditation on Psalm 119:19, Dietrich had written: "The earth, which nourishes me, has a right to my work and my strength. I have no right to despise the earth on which I live. I owe it loyalty and gratitude. It is my lot to be a stranger and a sojourner, but this cannot become a reason for evading God's call so that I dream away my earthly life with thoughts of heaven. There is a very godless homesickness for the other world which is not consistent with really finding one's home there. I ought to behave myself like a guest here, with all that entails. I should not stay aloof and refuse to participate in the tasks, joys and sorrows of earth, while I am waiting patiently for the redemption of the divine promise. I am really to wait for the promise and not try to steal it in advance in wishes and dreams."

Waiting patiently is a virtue when that for which we hope cannot be grasped or even seen in the present. If there is a godless homesickness for a future world, as Dietrich wrote, then there is also a godly homesickness. The godless desire for a future world despises the present world or, if that desire comes to frustration, turns to this world as the solution to the longing for a future. This is what produced an Ishmael. Godly homesickness is created by God not by our own desire. The longing for a world free of pain and struggle, a promised land, can only exist when God places that longing in our hearts. Abraham had a desire for an heir. God placed in him a seed of hope that could only come through his barren wife, Sarah. That longing gave way to a desire which sought immediate fulfillment. Abraham could not endure waiting for the promise to be fulfilled in God's time and in God's way. When one's endurance comes to an end, one's patience comes to an end.

There are two words in the Greek New Testament that are often translated as patience. One is *makroth*, which means forbearance or long-suffering. This word is only used twice. In the book of Hebrews it is used to encourage us to diligence in order to realize the full assurance of hope by imitating those who through faith and patience inherited the promises (Heb 6:12). In somewhat the same way James reminds us of the prophets of old who exercised patience and suffering (James 5:10). The other word, *hupomone*, which means endurance or continuance, is used frequently both as related to humans and also of God. Peter attributes patience to the Lord while we wait for our salvation (2 Peter 3:15), and referred to the patience of God in the days of Noah (1 Peter 3:20). Paul also speaks of the patience that Jesus exhibited toward him while he was in rebellion as an example to others who might come to believe in him (1 Tim 1:16). Patience is a vital component of hope, for if we hope for what we do not see "we wait for it with patience" (Rom 8:25). James tells us that patience (endurance) results from our faith being tested so that its effect might produce maturity (James 1:4). When we turn to the virtue of patience as it is related to the hope that comes only from God, we will discover that patience is more of a gift than a personality trait. In fact, as Paul tells us, it is a "fruit of the Spirit" (Gal 5:22).

Hopeful Patience

The patience that comes from hope is a special kind of patience. It is a 'hopeful patience.' Hope creates patience; patience by itself does not lead to hope. The patience that hope creates is like a mother waiting for the child conceived within her to come to full term. This patient waiting has both a promising beginning and a promise-filled future. This is why the patience of hope is more than simply enduring a difficult, painful or merely empty time, waiting until it is over. Thus, the words used to speak of this patience in Scripture do not by etymology alone denote the kind of patience that hope creates. One must suspend the waiting for hope within the promise of hope, and not allow impatience to rob hope of its own fulfillment. This is what Abraham discovered with regard to his Ishmael, and what the disciples of Jesus discovered while waiting for the promise of Pentecost.

Before Jesus left his disciples following the forty days after his resurrection, he told them to stay in Jerusalem and to "wait there for the promise of the Father." They wanted to know how long it would be and when it would come, revealing already their impatience. Jesus replied, "It is not for you to know the times or periods that the Father has set by his own authority" (Acts 1:4, 7). They were to wait for the coming of the Holy Spirit that would empower them for witness and mission.

They had not yet grasped the fact that waiting for God's promise is not a time to be filled with their own activity, but is a time already filled with expectation. Waiting is not 'lost time,' but 'hopeful time.' But they grew impatient. And Peter finally called a meeting in order to get something on the agenda. He told the other disciples that with the death of Judas there were now only eleven and there ought to be twelve, as originally specified by Jesus. As a result of Peter's suggestion, they went about setting their own criteria for who might be a successor to Judas and after narrowing the list down to two, they cast lots in order to discern which one should be chosen. The assumption was that through the random casting of lots it would give Jesus a chance to make the final selection. It did not seem to occur to them that in rejecting all of the candidates but two, they had already ruled out someone that Jesus might have wanted! When the lot was cast, Matthias was chosen to be the twelfth apostle (Acts 1:15-26). There is no further reference to him as one of the apostles and no indication that this was God's purpose and plan. It could well be that Matthias turned out to be their Ishmael. Meanwhile, after Pentecost and the coming of the Holy Spirit, Saul of Tarsus was apprehended by Jesus himself on the road to Damascus and by Jesus own choice, became an apostle (Acts 9; Gal 1).

The fact that Dietrich Bonhoeffer was able to express hopeful patience in spite of the depressing circumstances of his imprisonment in contrast with his fiancé, Maria, may be due to his earlier writing on the relation of the ultimate to the penultimate, or the 'last things' and the 'next to the last.' In the posthumous publication of his writings on *Ethics*, he wrote that the coming of Christ and the resurrection would be the final, or ultimate Word. We have assurance that this will occur, he said, by the fact of Christ's own resurrection. Resurrection is the 'last Word.' Our Christian life of faith is lived out during the penultimate time, before the ultimate Word. Because we know that there is an ultimate, or final answer to the questions that faith asks, we live in the penultimate time waiting for this final Word. The tendency, he wrote, is to attempt (through impatience) to pull the ultimate into the penultimate and in so doing rob the penultimate of its own meaning and significance. We cannot enter into the time of human suffering with only the ultimate Word at our disposal. We know the ultimate Word. It is the final Word. It is the Word of the gospel. But it cannot be 'spoken' in the time of the penultimate in such a way that it destroys faith by making of faith an illusion or even a mockery of the promise. "Does one not in some cases, by remaining deliberately in the penultimate, perhaps point all the more genuinely to the ultimate, which God will speak in His own time (though indeed through a human mouth)." He went on to explain this by saying that there is no penultimate in itself. A period of time can become penultimate only when the ultimate is known. The penultimate does not determine the ultimate, it is the ultimate that determines the ultimate.

For example, if I were to ask, "What is the next to the last number in this series?" and then to count beginning with the number 1, there could be no possible right answer. But if I were to say that the number 7 is the last number in a series, then the number 6 can immediately be known to be the next to the last. One might use this to explain why the seventh day was determined by God to be the last day in the story of creation and why the seventh day was to be hallowed and remembered as the day that marked the 'completion' of God's creative work. Because this 'sabbath' has been revealed through the death and resurrection of Jesus Christ we know that it is the final Word that awaits consummation. We live by faith, waiting for the promise, during the next to the last (penultimate) time. This is why the author of the book of Hebrews warns us not to be disobedient and rebellious, but to eagerly await the entering into this eternal rest. "So then a Sabbath rest still remains for the people of God" (Heb 4:9). We are living in the penultimate time, waiting for the ultimate by "holding fast to our confession" (Heb. 4:14). Bonhoeffer wrote, "For the sake of the ultimate the penultimate must be preserved. Any arbitrary destruction of the penultimate will do serious injury to the ultimate." The penultimate time is not a time of mere passive waiting, but it is a time of "preparing the way of the Lord."

The Creative Work of Patience

Patience is not just 'killing time,' it is "redeeming the time" (Eph 5:16; Col 4:5, KJV). The same word is used by Paul for redeeming the time as used in speaking of Christ redeeming us from the curse of the law (Gal 4:13). To 'redeem time' as used in this context is to deliver time from the fate of 'time' by connecting the penultimate time to the ultimate time of God's redemption of all things. This is why the author of the book of Hebrews exhorts us not to just passively wait for the last day of eternal rest, but to "make every effort" to enter into that rest (Heb 4:11). Waiting for the hope that comes from God is a penultimate time of sowing, caring, pruning, and watering, as I have explored in the preceding chapters. The growing season is often the busiest time for a gardener, and often for a farmer. Harvest is a highly active but brief period in the season of hope. By using this analogy to depict the life of hope and spiritual power in the midst of daily life, we see how important it is to do the creative work of hope as partners of God while waiting for the ultimate Word to arrive as the culmination (harvest) of redemptive history.

For Dietrich Bonhoeffer the impatience and frustration shown by Maria was not only a waste of time, it was just 'killing time.' Did he not also long for freedom? Was he not also envisioning this terrible time coming to an end so that he could complete what he had lived for? Of course. But this longing and hope was not something that destroyed his present (penultimate) time. In fact, the two years in prison, while representing the final time of his life (he was executed just prior to the end of the war), became his most creative time. His activity in reading, writing and ministry to others in prison became a 'full-time' occupation. We only reflect upon and ponder the brilliant insights of his theological mind and the passionate and powerful confession of his faith due to these letters from prison. After the war Maria immigrated to the United States, experienced two failed marriages and directed that her correspondence with Dietrich only be released after her death. In the narrative of her life, the brief engagement to Dietrich is little more than a paragraph. Her longing for him was never fulfilled; it could never become the creative work that it was for him.

Elizabeth Barrett Browning, writing of her own love wrote: "How do I love thee? Let me count the ways./... I love thee with a love I seemed to lose/ With my lost saints,--I love thee with the breath,' Smiles, tears, of all my life!—and if God choose,' I shall but love thee better after death."

The days of waiting do count, when hope lies on the other side of time. The Psalmist wrote, "Teach us to count our days that we may gain a wise heart" (Ps 90:12). I never counted the days until harvest, and if asked what day the harvest would begin I had to say, I do not know. The harvest begins only when the harvest is ready. Every day points forward and each day has its own meaning and purpose because of the ultimate day when the harvest is gathered. The creative work of patience lies on this side of the ultimate. The harvest brings the end of patience and the beginning of a new kind of creative life in the eternal Word of God. I enjoy this hope everyday.

Part Three
FALL

The Harvest of Hope

Scott
October 4, 1994

Few are the days and many the years
  that bind our hearts in common birth.
Precarious and precious, the moment nears
  when we are destined to meet on earth
        face to face.

What will we say? What language shall we use
  to loosen our tongues and set our spirits aflame?
Strangers, yet kin, we can be friends if we choose
  to meet with open face; speaking each other's name
        with kindly grace.

Catch in my eyes a distant glimpse of Dakota skies,
  and see the flash of light as thunder clouds form.
Feel the stir in my soul when the wild geese cries,
  and stay with me through the coming storm,
        that hides my face.

There is too little time for us to tame;
  there are too many stories to tell.
You will see my face and hear my name,
  but only in heaven come to know me well
        face to face.

When you awaken to find your special place,
  and know that God has chosen well;
When you see your soul in another's face,
  then you will hear what I tried to tell,
        you are Scott!
                              RSA

Chapter 9 - Timing
Don't Wait for it to Fall in Your Lap

As harvest approached on the farm, I was always anxious to have it begin. It was usually preceded by a daily ritual where my father walked out into the grain field, shelling a few kernels in his hand, sometimes biting into the seed to test its hardness, and then making his pronouncement. "We will have to a wait a few days." Or, much more exciting to me, "It's ready, we will begin first thing in the morning, if it doesn't rain."

Determining the right time, with regard to wheat, for example, had to do with the moisture content. Actually, even in those days, one could take a small sample into town where the local grain elevator had equipment to test the moisture content. But I always figured that my father trusted his own method better than to depend on some reading provided by an instrument. Today, of course, the modern grain combines provide instant read-outs of moisture content as the grain is being harvested. Very efficient, but have we lost something in losing the ritual of father and son walking into the grain field in the evening? Probably. But this may be a minor loss compared to the separation of our souls from the soil when harvesting has become more like shopping.

It becomes increasingly difficult to understand, much less apply, the figures of speech and parables of Jesus to our everyday life. In biblical times, everyone lived by the seasons and took account of the times. Listen to the words of Jesus. "Do you not say, 'Four months more then comes the harvest?' But I tell you, look around you, and see how the fields are ripe for harvesting" (John 4:35). Most everything changes color when it matures (even the hair on our head!). Wheat changes from green to golden; oats from green to white. Those who live by the harvest know how to read the signs. Timing is every thing, not only with hitting a baseball, but with gathering a harvest. Those who heard this saying of Jesus knew instantly what he meant. The time when God's salvation was understood to belong only to the children of Israel was over. The seed sown through the descendents of Abraham was intended to produce a harvest from "all the families of the earth" (Gen 12:3).

The immediate context of Jesus' words was the remarkable encounter that Jesus had with the woman of Samaria. "God is spirit," Jesus told her in response to her rather provocative challenge concerning the proper place to worship, "and those who worship must worship in spirit and truth" (John 4:24). Her witness to her own people that she had found the promised Messiah indicated that it was harvest time. The 'field' that was ripe for harvesting was the Samaritans who came to believe in him through her words (John 4:39-42). Who did the harvesting in that incident? Some might be quick to say, "It was Jesus, of course." But they would be wrong. The Samaritan woman was not merely a convert harvested by Jesus, she reaped a harvest among her own people. The point of Jesus' saying this to the disciples was, in effect, "Go and do likewise."

Harvesting Hope

We have been speaking of hope. There are many levels of hope, but every hope is a promise of a harvest. We can plan a picnic and hope for a sunny day. If it does not rain, and the picnic is a success, we have 'harvested that hope.' But even here, such a mundane thing as a picnic requires some planning and the execution of the plan. "If it does not rain," is the contingency that is outside of our control. If it is a church picnic we might be encouraged by the Pastor to pray for nice weather, assuming that the spiritual component (control of the weather) belongs to God. Thus we do our part by planning the picnic and leave God's part to answer our prayer for nice weather.

In this illustration two things emerge. First, we have separated the spiritual aspect of hope (prayer for a nice day) from the human aspect, plan for the picnic, buy the hot dogs and drinks, and arrange for transportation. Secondly, we have divided the work between two agents: God is the agent who works with the weather, we are the agent who actually does the work for the picnic. Is this not a normal way to think of how God works in our lives? If God does not answer our prayer for a nice day, we always have plan B: move the picnic inside. Because God was only the agent who controlled the weather, through our own agency, we can 'harvest' the hope of having a picnic, though it might be a bit inconvenient due to the rain. As to why God did not answer our prayer for a nice day, that can be set aside as a theological question for those not planning picnics to worry (and write books!) about.

Well, if this is the normal pattern of our everyday spiritual life, it might work with regard to picnics but not so well when it comes to the work of the Kingdom of God. And after all, the Kingdom of God as Jesus taught it and the Apostle Paul viewed it, was an everyday work of God by which through our human lives, the Kingdom is expanded by the 'harvest' of persons for Kingdom living.

Expanding God's Kingdom on earth is no picnic. We cannot separate the work of the Kingdom into two eras—this present age and the age to come—leaving the harvest go until the end of this age, meanwhile, planning our own picnics. It does not work that way. Through Jesus the future age has entered into the present age, and the time for harvest has already come. What does this mean? It means that we can no longer think in terms of two separate agents—God who deals with the supernatural, and humans who work within the natural. There are, in fact, two agents, God and humans. It is just that we cannot parcel out the work of the Kingdom as we do when planning a picnic so that when God does not perform his work, we simply move our work inside out of the weather.

The problem of how God as an agent is responsible for the harvest and we humans responsible to 'bring in the harvest' is not just a problem for theologians, it is a structure of reality than requires a theological understanding.

The Apostle Paul described this clearly, using again the analogy of sowing and reaping. "We are only God's servants through whom you believed the Good News. Each of us did the work the Lord gave us. I planted the seed in your hearts, and Apollos watered it, but it was God who made it grow. It's not important who does the planting or who does the watering. What's important is that God makes the seed grow. The one who plants and the one who waters work together with the same purpose. And both will be rewarded for their own hard work. For we are both God's workers. And you are God's field. You are God's building" (1 Cor 3:5-9 NLT).

While Paul clearly indicated that God as the agent of creation and redemption is the ultimate source of the entire work, not only the harvest, humans have their work to do in order that the harvest is gathered. Ben Quash explains this by using the analogy of the production of a dramatic work. He suggests that divine and human agency do not compete with each other but rather, but following the analogy of a play, the author and the actor are part of a single action. The one who acts does not replace the agency of the one who writes; rather, the writer empowers the actor and the actor releases the power of the writer. He says: "Drama offers a sort of parable of the fact that the exercise of power resides at least partially in letting other people act. The secret is not to suppose that your agency

is incompatible with the agency of others--that there is competition for a
limited 'space' of agency. Your agency does not need to push the agency
of others aside in order to triumph.... Just so, in dealing with the Christian
God, we ought not to be in the business of identifying which actions are
our achievements, and which God's puppetry, in order to attribute relative quantities of power respectively.... The highest instance of power we
have been given to know in the God of Jesus Christ does not compete for
a limited arena so that it can exercise itself in brute solitude over against
us."

I like that analogy. I would push it a bit further to suggest that God
has not just written a script for actors to perform, but is a writer/director
so that the production is open to some improvisation. I think that Jesus
'improvised' when confronted with the Samaritan woman's response.
His 'timing' was perfect. She tried to prolong the 'game' by introducing
the age-old controversy between the Jews and Samaritans with regard to
the proper place to worship. He saw what she was doing and cut 'right
to the chase,' as we say, by telling her that it is a matter of the spirit, not
of geography. He saw the fruit was ripe for picking and reached out and
took it. But then when she herself became a witness to her own people,
suddenly she became the agent who gathered the harvest. Even so they
confessed, "It is no longer because of what you said that we believe, for
we have heard for ourselves, and we know that this is truly the Savior of
the world" (John 4:42). Isn't that a nice transition? She and Jesus are not
competing for the same role, as Quash said, but Jesus allowed her to act,
while in the end he is the true agent of salvation. He is the Lord of the
harvest. He does not wait for it to fall in his lap, but sends out agents to
do the harvesting.

Hands-Off Spirituality

I have met Christians who are so anxious to preserve their salvation
by grace alone, that they take a hands-off approach. Because God is the
agent of their salvation and it is only through grace, not by the works of
the law, they live in fear of undermining grace by attempting to achieve
righteousness through their own efforts. Their hope of salvation is rightly
in what Christ has achieved for them through his own life of obedience
unto death on the cross and his resurrection. Nothing can be added to that.
Salvation is a gift of God (John 1:12). We should keep our own hands off
and depend solely upon God to bestow it upon us. Some day, by this way
of thinking, if we do nothing but depend only upon the grace of God, it
will fall right into our laps.

Some attempt to practice this 'hands-off' spirituality even with regard the ordering of their daily life. A man came into my office when I was pastor of a church, seeking some counsel with regard to a vocational decision. "I feel the Lord leading me to change jobs," he told me, "but nothing seems to be happening. My wife and I have prayed about this for several months now, but I have no assurance from the Lord as to what direction to look." When I inquired as to the reasons for thinking that he should change jobs, he replied; "My present salary is not sufficient to meet our needs, and we are expecting another child. My job does not really match my vocational training, and I really need to get into another line of work."

It became clear as I probed further about attempts he had already made to find another job that he had so spiritualized the situation that any thought of making aggressive moves toward finding other employment appeared to be a lack of faith. He admitted that he had asked the Lord for a 'fleece,' citing the passage in the book of Judges chapter six, where Gideon sought assurance that the Lord was really going to deliver the Israelites as he had promised. Gideon laid out a 'fleece of wool' and told the Lord that if, in the morning, the fleece was wet with dew while the ground all around was dry, he would have certainty that the Lord would deliver Israel by his hand. In the morning, the fleece was wet, but the ground was dry. Gideon was not done! He said to the Lord, I want to try it once more, and this time if the fleece is dry while the ground all around is wet I will know that you will deliver Israel by my hand. In the morning, the fleece was dry and Gideon concluded that he should go ahead and lead the Israelite troops into battle (Judges 6:36-40). It was this Scripture story that the man had seized upon as a means of determining that it would be the Lord rather than his own efforts, to secure a better job. "I went ahead on my own when I got this job," he told me, "and it was clearly a mistake. This time I want the Lord to show me what he wants me to do."

This was not the first time that I had heard of 'fleecing' in order to determine the will of God in a practical matter of everyday life. When I suggested to this man that he find some one whose profession it was to place a person in a new job, he was rather scandalized. Not only did he feel that this was a secular and unspiritual way to go about such an important decision, but it became clear that his very salvation seemed to be at stake in taking such an action by his own hand. In working with him, it was necessary to go back and reconstruct his understanding of grace with regard to salvation. The way in which we understand our role in working with God to achieve what he has promised is crucial to the way in which we seek to implement spirituality into everyday life.

In the quotation from Ben Quash cited above, he suggested that God as the primary agent who works out our salvation through Christ does not compete with us with regard to our agency. We are not to place all of the spiritual aspect of our hope for salvation on God. That would rule out our participation in the 'drama' of our redemption. We are also composing the script for the narrative of our life through our decisions and actions. In the story of their lives as agents of God, the biblical characters in the drama do not hand off to God the realization of their hopes, expecting it to fall in their laps. They devise plans, work out strategy, and act as though the outcome depends upon what they accomplish, even though in the end, they confess that it was the Lord who enabled them to achieve the goal.

One of my favorite stories in the Bible is the one where Abraham sent his servant back to the land of his ancestors to find a wife for his son Isaac. The servant asked a very realistic question, not how to find the right one but, what if she is unwilling to come back here to marry Isaac? Abraham replied, in that case you are free from your vow, just do not take my son back there for my son to find a wife. "But if the woman is unwilling to follow you, then you shall be free from this oath of mine." Abraham told the servant, "The Lord, before whom I walk, will send his angel with you and make your way successful" (Gen 24:7-8; 40). But it is not going to be that simple! The angel depended upon the servant to execute the plan. Here we have multiple agency, both divine and human. Abraham is one agent who issues the order to his servant, who became an agent in his own right. The Lord is the agent whom Abraham trusts to fulfill his hope that a wife for Isaac can be found, who works through the agency of an angel. The woman is her own agent, allowed to make her own decision.

Could God have presented a woman to Isaac to be his wife through a series of providential and supernatural moves that left out the human factor altogether? I suppose so, if one thinks of God as the only agent in the drama. But what would be the point? Humans would be mere puppets in God's hand. Of what value is a theology that seeks to preserve God's power at the expense of human participation? Does a view of divine providence yield more honor to God because it leaves out human freedom and human participation? The man who came to me for pastoral counsel with respect to his future career seemed to think so. But the biblical narratives that tell of God's agency in fulfilling our hope do not lead us to that conclusion. A 'hands-off' spirituality is not only frustrating and futile, it is not biblical. It is not the way God works.

What I find fascinating is that Abraham is convinced that God will work through his servant allowing for him to work out the strategy to fulfill the vow and allowing the woman he contacts the freedom to make her own decision. When the servant worked out a strategy for selecting a wife for Isaac, Rebecca agreed to accompany him back and marry Isaac. The servant, having worked out his own plan for finding the woman, concluded, "the Lord led me by the right way" (Gen 24:48). It is only in retrospect that both the divine and human agency comes together in such a way that both can be seen working 'hand-in-hand' to bring forth what neither could do alone.

Hand-in-Hand Spirituality

Those who seem to find in the Apostle Paul the proof texts for their view of a 'hands-off' spirituality can readily find them if that is what they are looking for. "And we have come to believe in Christ Jesus, so that we might be justified by faith in Christ, and not by doing the works of the law, because no one will be justified by the works of the law" (Gal 2:16). Justification as Paul used the term, meant to be declared righteous before God. Abraham, said Paul, "believed God, and it was reckoned to him as righteousness." He went on to use the analogy of a worker who is paid wages. "Now to one who works, wages are not reckoned as a gift but as something due" (Rom 4:3-4). Referring to the promise made to Abraham that he would have an inheritance through a son (Isaac), Paul said that the realization of this promise rested on faith so that it might come through grace and so be guaranteed to all his descendants (Rom 4:16). The implication can be drawn from this text that Abraham was declared righteous and received the promise only because he had faith and not because of his own work.

And yet, we have just heard the story of how Abraham actually received the promise. It did not 'fall into his lap,' so to speak, as a sovereign gift from God apart from the human agency involved. True, the promise was not given to Abraham due to the merit of his religious keeping of a law (this is Paul's main point). However, as we have seen, human agency was involved along with human freedom in such a way that a wonderful 'human drama' resulted in which both divine and human agency worked 'hand-in-hand' to produce the result.

It is therefore wrong to take the text of Paul regarding the righteousness of faith through grace as contrasted with the righteousness sought by human effort alone as the basis for a 'hands-off- spirituality. Even with regard to our salvation that comes through faith by grace, and Paul has personal experience of this, we are human agents in working out this gift of salvation. "Therefore, my beloved, just as you have always obeyed me, not only in my presence, but much more now in my absence, work out your own salvation with fear and trembling; for it is God who is at work in you, enabling you both to will and to work for his good pleasure" (Phil 2:12-13). Here again, we have the dual agency, both divine and human, working 'hand-in-hand' through grace to receive the hope of salvation that can only come from God.

In the dramatic story of Paul's journey by ship from Caesarea to Rome as a prisoner, in order to appeal to Caesar, a storm threatened the ship. Paul had earlier warned the captain that the season for winter storms was close and they should not depart from the port of Fair Havens (Acts 27:9-12). The Captain ignored this warning and set sail, only to find that Paul was right. They were caught in a terrible storm that threatened to sink the ship. Paul reminded the captain that he had warned against just such a catastrophe and announced, "Last night there stood by me an angel of the God to whom I belong and whom I worship, and he said, 'Do not be afraid, Paul; you must stand before the emperor; and indeed, God has granted safety to all those who are sailing with you.'" Paul went on to say, "So keep up your courage, men, for I have faith in God that it will be exactly as I have been told. But we will have to run aground on some island" (Acts 27:13-16).

Here again, as with the story of Abraham and his servant, we have multiple agents. Paul has his own role to play; though a prisoner he has some influence with the captain. The captain commands the ship and his word is final. An angel of God appeared to Paul with the promise of eventual safety. Paul added his own commentary by saying, 'It looks like a shipwreck on an island is our only hope.' The story continues. As they near an island and the ship began to break up, all of the sailors began to abandon ship, whereupon Paul said, "Unless these men say in the ship, you cannot be saved" (Acts 27:31). As it turned out, the ship did break up on the rocks, and all escaped safely to shore. All hands on deck, is not only a call to action when there is a storm at sea. It is a summons to turn prayer into action and contemplation into commitment.

So how do we approach the harvest of hope? Do we just pray and then sit back and wait for it to fall in our laps? It does not seem to work that way. Even near the end of his life Paul kept advancing, kept fighting, kept running. "So I do not run aimlessly, nor do I box as though beating the air, but I punish my body and enslave it, so that after proclaiming to others I myself should not be disqualified" (1 Cor 9:26-27).

It is a matter of timing. As a gymnast lets go of the high bar and hurtles through the air toward the outstretched hands of a partner, both join hands only if their timing is accurate. So it is with God's hand and ours.

We better not be daydreaming with folded hands while God is reaching out into our lives with his.

When Lucy, in the Peanuts comic strip, lets a fly ball drop right in front of her during the baseball game, Charlie Brown rushes out to her and demanded an explanation. "I was having my devotions," she said. As the preacher said in the book of Ecclesiastes, "There is a time to plant and a time to pluck up what is planted" (Ecc 3:2).

The harvest that waits in the field is not yet a harvest. Sower and reaper only rejoice together when what is reaped is gathered. That may take more than one hand.

Chapter 10 - Reaping

It Isn't a Harvest Until You Take it Home

We were standing around in the local John Deere shop in our small town when the owner said to my father, "Looks like you've got a good harvest this year." My father replied, "It's a good crop, but it's not a harvest until I get it home." Not every good crop resulted in a good harvest; my father knew that from experience. The few weeks around harvest time are critical. Strong winds, hail, and even too much rain can ruin in a few hours what it took an entire summer to produce. Grain standing in a field waiting to be harvested is beautiful to the eye, but until it is safely stored in a bin at home, it is wise not to spend the money it represents. "Don't count your chickens before they are hatched," my father once said to a young farmer who was broadcasting around town his intention to buy a new tractor with the corn crop that he was expecting to harvest in the fall. Is there spiritual wisdom in all of this? You bet there is.

The metaphor of reaping a harvest is one of the oldest in the biblical tradition. In the original Garden of Eden planting and harvesting are part of the creation mandate given to humans. "God said, 'See I have given you every plant yielding seed that is upon the face of the earth, and every tree with seed in its fruit; you shall have them for food'" (Gen 1:29). Every aspect of human life as intended by the Creator is the workplace in which humans experience simultaneously their spiritual and material existence. Their spiritual life does not divide the workplace into secular and sacred spheres, as though Adam and Eve had to withdraw from their material existence into some separate place in order to have a spiritual relation to the Creator.

The Spirituality of Everyday Life

Human nature is both material and spiritual. As originally created, humans experience their spiritual life as freely and fully as they do their material life, along with other creatures placed upon the earth. What constitutes spiritual life for Adam and Eve is not in contrast to or separate from their material life. Rather, their material or creaturely existence is spiritual at the very core.

The original intrinsic relation of humans to the soil from which their daily living came, and to each other as well as to God, was broken in the Fall away from God's grace by the first humans. What was originally a daily sacrament of divine partnership and human fellowship was shattered at the core, leaving humans estranged from God, alienated from the earth from which came their sustenance, and living in fear of one another. Contrary to conventional thinking, the humans were never cursed, but their relation to the earth was fractured. "Cursed is the ground because of you; in toil you shall eat of it all the days of your life. Thorns and thistles it shall bring for you; and you shall eat the plants of the field. By the sweat of your face you shall eat bread until you return to the ground, for out of it you were taken; you are dust, and to dust you shall return" (Gen 3:17-19). Even here we are reminded that the earth is not the enemy. There will now be frustration and failure—not every crop will result in a harvest—yet bringing the harvest home is still both a material and a spiritual metaphor of hope.

What remains intact, despite the result of the Fall, is the original symbiotic relation between God, the earth and human life. I cited earlier (Chapter Eight) the mediation on Psalm 119 by Dietrich Bonhoeffer, "The earth, which nourishes me, has a right to my work and my strength. I have no right to despise the earth on which I live. I owe it loyalty and gratitude." This is why the analogy of sowing and reaping carries such spiritual significance. When our spiritual life becomes primarily a religious attitude and activity, separated from our daily life, hope becomes more fragile and unreal to the degree that it becomes entirely spiritual. And without spiritual content, our daily life 'under the sun', as the author of Ecclesiastes tells us, is hopeless; "all is vanity and a chasing after wind" (Ecc 4:4).

The hope of salvation for the people of Israel was eschatological, that is, it was something that awaited the day of the Lord, a future event. Nonetheless, this salvation was pictured in their minds as a redemption of earthly living. Hope of salvation was not merely a hope of being liberated from this earthly body, so that an immortal soul could be released. This was the prevailing Greek philosophy at the time that the Old Testament prophets wrote. For the Hebrews, life was bound to the earth and their soul to the body; their hope of redemption was not in some unearthly existence but in the redemption of earth and therefore their life on earth.

The prophetic vision was in a harvest that bought hope home in the form of a transformed earthly life. "The wilderness and the dry land shall be glad, the desert shall rejoice and blossom," sang the prophet (Isa 35:1). This was a vision that brought hope home to the blind and oppressed. "Then the eyes of the blind shall be opened, and the ears of the deaf unstopped; then the lame shall leap like a deer and the tongue of the speechless sing for joy" (Isa 35:5-6). The song was one of hope for those who were victims of brutality and captives in a strange land. "A highway shall be there and it shall be called the Holy Way; . . .No lion shall be there, nor shall any ravenous beast come up on it. . . And the ransomed of the Lord shall return, and come to Zion with singing" (Isa 35:8, 9, 10). Hope of salvation is to be brought home to a place that is free from pain, suffering and where everything is restored to the way that God the Creator intended.

With this vision of hope passed on from generation to generation, we can now understand the significance that people saw in the words and actions of Jesus. He brought hope home by healing the sick, giving sight to the blind, casting out of demons, and creating a place where a woman who was unclean due to a continuing issue of blood could find a 'clean place,' a Holy Way, in which to experience hope (Luke 8:43-48). The final prophetic vision is cast in terms of a new heaven and a new earth, where "The home of God is among mortals. He will dwell with them; they will be his peoples, and God himself will be with them; he will wipe every tear from their eyes. Death will be no more; mourning and crying and pain will be no more, for the first things have passed away" (Rev 21:1-4). Jesus himself promised that he will prepare a place for us, a home where we can come and be with him and with those who belong to us (John 14:2-3).

Yes, I know, these images are metaphors, but they are metaphors that convey a message. Hope is not something that exists somewhere outside of and beyond our earthly life. Rather, hope is God's salvation that can be 'brought home' to us in our present time, even as a sacrament or sign of an eternal hope that overcomes and transforms our mortal life.

Bringing The Harvesting of Hope Home

So how do we 'bring the harvest of hope home' when its fullness lies beyond this temporal life? This is where the redemption of this present age enters in as a kind of sacrament of hope. I use the word 'sacrament' here as a way of binding the eternal to the temporal in such a way that the spiritual reality of hope can be grasped and experienced in the midst of our everyday, secular life. Earlier in this chapter, I referred to the 'sacrament' of divine participation in the 'workplace' where the first humans lived before the Fall. Their life was not divided into secular and religious spheres as though their spiritual connection to the Creator as the life-line of hope could only be experienced by withdrawing from secular work into religious worship. What later became a religious sacrament administered by a priestly caste, was at first a 'secular sacrament' where work and worship were part of daily existence. In this sense, when God entered in to meet with them at the 'time of the evening breeze,' hope as divine promise was brought home to them by divine presence (Gen 3:8).

The incarnation of the divine Son of God into human form in the person of Jesus of Nazareth, began the process of redeeming the secular sphere from the effects of the Fall. Jesus was then, in effect, a sacrament by which divine presence and human existence were bound together in such a way that "in him the whole fullness of deity dwells bodily." Paul adds , "and you have come to fullness in him" (Col 2:9-10). This is why Paul also could say that the religious significance of the Sabbath as only one day of the week has now become a spiritual reality in Christ by which hope can be experienced (brought home) every day (Rom 14:5-6).

But let us think of this in more practical terms. If, as the prophets said, when the 'day of the Lord' has come, then justice, mercy, health, personal well-being and peace will come 'on earth as it is in heaven;' the harvest of hope is brought home when this transformation begins to occur. This was announced by Jesus as a sign that the Messiah would come when he gave his first talk in a synagogue. This was following his baptism at which time the Spirit descended upon him (anointed him). The Spirit descending upon Jesus represented the fulfillment of the promise that the Spirit of God would anoint one to usher in the Day of the Lord wherein salvation would come to the people of God. The popular name for this expected savior was Messiah, taken from the Hebrew word for anointing (*mashach*, to anoint; *mishchah*, anointed). A typical passage from the Old Testament prophecies of this event can be found in Isaiah 61:1-2, a passage from which Jesus read in the synagogue in Nazareth. "The spirit of the Lord is upon me, because he has anointed me to bring good news to the poor. He has sent me to proclaim release to the captives, and recovery of sight to the blind, to let the oppressed go free, to proclaim the year of the Lord's favor." Immediately after reading this passage, Jesus said, "Today this scripture has been fulfilled in your hearing" (Luke 4:16-21).

By identifying himself as the anointed one to which this prophetic word pointed, Jesus, for the first time, accepted the designation as Messiah. The Greek translation of the Hebrew word Messiah is *Christus.* Jesus of Nazareth from this point can also be called the Christ, the Messiah, one anointed by the Spirit of God to carry out the ministry of God and bring hope to the hopeless. In his miracles of deliverance and ministry to the poor, Jesus brought the harvest of hope home, even though it was the 'first fruits' of the harvest and not the entirety of it.

In drawing persons around him, Jesus re-created humanity in the form of a community of shared life and common identity. Even this narrower circle, defined by the specific calling of the twelve, was structurally open to the 'unclean leper,' the tormented demoniac, the self-righteous Pharisee, and the women of ambiguous reputation. In contact with Jesus, humanity was liberated from the blind and capricious powers of nature and disease, as well as from the cruel and inhuman practices of the social and religious tyranny of the powerful over the weak. In the real humanity of Jesus we see the humanization as well as the socialization of humanity.

The third-century theologian, Irenaeus, wrote concerning the Spirit of God: "For God promised, that in the last times He would pour Him [the Spirit] upon His servants and handmaids, that they might prophesy; wherefore He did also descend upon the Son of God, made the Son of man, becoming accustomed in fellowship with Him to dwell in the human race, to rest with human beings, and to dwell in the workmanship of God, working the will of the Father in them, and renewing them from their old habits into the newness of Christ." Jesus brought the Spirit 'home' in a way of speaking by allowing the Spirit to enter into his total humanity, so that the Holy Spirit now is 'accustomed to dwell in the human race.'

Through the Holy Spirit that Jesus sent following his resurrection and ascension, the future hope of redemption was multiplied through the gifts and fruit of the Spirit. One might well say after hearing Paul proclaim the good news of the Kingdom, "That sounds like a good harvest." But Paul would respond, "It is not a harvest until you bring it home." One can applaud the good news of the gospel as announced in a sermon, but it is not yet a harvest. The fruit of the Spirit is not a religious expression of faith, but a transforming experience of hope. What the Apostle Paul calls the 'works of the flesh' as contrasted with the 'fruit of the Spirit,' are symptomatic of negative and pathological social spirituality. There is hope for those tormented by "fornication, impurity, licentiousness, idolatry, sorcery, enmities, strife, jealousy, anger, quarrels, dissension, factions, envy, drunkenness, carousing, and things like that" (Gal 5:19-21). But these vicious and inhuman forces that creep into most every life and relationship do not disappear merely through religious ritual. Religion itself can be mean and abusive when used to further one's own interests rather than to fulfill God's purpose for humanity. Jesus' strongest words of warning and even condemnation were spoken to the religious leaders of his day who used the Law of Moses virtually as a club to beat persons into submission. What the Apostle Paul describes as the 'works of the flesh' as contrasted with the 'fruit of the Spirit,' are symptomatic of negative and pathological social spirituality. These are some of the diagnostic categories by which the Bible identifies sin; not first of all violations of an abstract moral law, but the breakdown of the social spirituality which is necessary for healthy marriage and family life, as well as other social relations.

The therapeutic effects of the indwelling of the Holy Spirit are likewise described in terms of healthy social spirituality--love, joy, peace, patience, kindness, generosity, faithfulness, gentleness, self-control (Gal 5:22-23). This fruit is only harvested when it is put into practice at home, in domestic settings and personal relationships, when carried home and lived out as the 'first fruits' of a coming harvest at the end of the age. I could give a sermon on the positive values that the fruit of the Spirit contribute to human life, but one ought to follow me home to ask those who live with me how far these virtues actually comprise the quality of my domestic and family life.

The transforming reality of the Spirit of Jesus when brought home, embraces whatever is broken and brings it toward wholeness. It touches whatever is orphaned and creates family. It saves families by saving husbands and wives from destroying each other through impossible ultimatums. It saves parents from having to determine their children's destinies, and it saves children from having to enshrine their parents in their own goals in order to honor them.

The Kingdom of God is a kingdom of hope. It cannot be equated with a religious institution or with mere religious practice. James speaks of bringing religion home in the form of spiritual empowerment for practical actions. "Pure and genuine religion in the sight of God the Father means caring for orphans and widows in their distress, and refusing to let the world corrupt you" (James 1:27 NLT). Kingdom living seeks to humanize humanity by transforming inhuman actions and situations by putting 'in place' here and now the redemption that is held in promise by hope. When we echo the cry of John the Baptist and sing, 'Prepare the way of the Lord,' we bring those words home when we make the 'crooked paths straight and the rough ways smooth' (Luke 3:4-5). For those who 'live in darkness,' the light will not shine on them until we bring it home (Isa 60:1-2). Jesus did not say, "I am the light of the world," while seated in the synagogue, but standing beside a man blind from birth (John 9:5).

In his letter to the Ephesian Christians, the apostle Paul drew out the implications of the gospel of Christ in such a way that the basic structures of that society were to be 'humanized' through the activation of the Spirit and law of Christ. Paul did not seek to replace their culture with a concept of a better 'religious culture.' Rather, he called for the liberation of authentic human life within the culture as a freedom from the 'magical' as well as from the mythical.

In this context, Paul provided a criterion of spiritual community that is grounded in the identification of Christ himself with those in whom his Holy Spirit dwells. Here too, both Jew and Gentile must learn to shift their obedience and loyalty from traditional concepts of authority by which they sought stability and order, to the structure of social life regulated by the community as the body of Christ (Eph 2:11-22). The foundational social structures of family, marriage, parents and children, as well as the existing political and economic structures are basically affirmed as good and necessary. Yet all of these structures are radically qualified by the 'humanization of humanity' which occurred through Jesus Christ (Eph 5, 6).

The Kingdom of God is the invisible sphere of Christ's power and reign into which we enter through the Holy Spirit and faith. In this way, Paul viewed the Kingdom of God as not primarily concerned with material things and political realms, but rather as a personal and social reality—righteousness and peace and joy—the fruits of the indwelling Spirit (Rom 14:17). Kingdom-living in the present time, according to Paul, begins with our reception of the Holy Spirit as the 'down payment' (*arrabon*) of our inheritance (Eph 1:14). The word signifies the promise of what lies in the future, and more than a promise, the present reality of living in that promise.

The 'harvest of the Spirit' does not occur just because we raise our hands in praise to God (that is spiritual worship), but more often when we 'give a hand' to one in need (that is spiritual living). There is a form of spiritual fanaticism that can be mistaken for the 'harvest of the spirit.' This can keep the harvest of hope at a distance, leaving us 'Spirit filled' but spiritually impoverished. It has been said that some are 'so heavenly minded that they are no earthly good.'

Bring the Spirit of hope home; don't be so full of the Spirit that your life at home is empty and fruitless. You will be thankful that you did. And then raise your hands in grateful worship. Gratitude makes a place for hope to live in the narrow places in our lives. Hope gets lonely when left in the guest room. Bring it in the family room.

Chapter 11 - Thanksgiving

Raising Hope With the Hands of Gratitude

There was a time when reaping was accompanied by rejoicing and 'bringing home the sheaves' followed by a time of thanksgiving. The reference of course, is to the Psalmist who recounts the joy of the exiles returning from captivity in Babylon, using the analogy of the joy of harvest. "May those who sow in tears reap with shouts of joy. Those who go out weeping, bearing the seed for sowing, shall come home with shouts of joy, carrying their sheaves" (Ps 126:5-6) Who could say today what is meant by 'sheaves,' or could imagine what it is like to shout with gratitude at harvest time. But I remember.

The sheaves are bundles of grain that were once upon a time cut with a hand-held blade, tied with strands of the cut grain into a bundle with the heads all on one end. I was shown how to do this by my father, as a way of transferring an art no longer needed from one generation to another. Is that itself not a lost art? I mean not how to tie up a bundle with stalks of grain, but the transfer of wisdom through rituals that once were necessary but now only quaint? I don't know what it is to have the kind of gratitude that could be wrapped by my own hands. Nor do I have the joy of harvesting what I have sown with my own hands. But I long for it. And the longing is itself a form of hope.

We harvested with a horse-drawn reaper that spit out the bundles already tied with mechanical fingers that I picked up and stacked neatly in small shocks of ten or twelve bundles each waiting to dry out for threshing. I have loaded these 'sheaves' into horse-drawn wagons, driven to the threshing machine, where they were tossed into the gaping maw of the roaring monster, heads first always, so that the slashing knives and spinning cylinders could separate the grain from the straw. I have stood, knee-deep in the threshed-out oats that had been gathered into the grain wagon, shoveling them into the granary bin at home, with greenish grasshoppers and angry black crickets swimming to the top of the ocean of oats, caught up unknowingly and unwillingly in their own harvest of death. Never mind. It was the sweet, warm smell of oats that stimulated my senses.

These are the sheaves that I gathered. And, while there were no actual shouts, the joy was there in broad smiles and hearty slaps on the back as we washed our sweaty arms and dusty faces in the outside pump by the well before sitting down before plates of freshly fried chicken and corn on the cob. Those were ancient tribal rituals where boys became men without being aware of it. But at times I was aware. And even now I shiver with excitement and swell with pride remembering the exhilarating joy of being one of them. We each can only remember what causes us to be who we are.

This is what my children will never know, and what I will carry to my grave. This is why thanksgiving has to be scheduled on the calendar and explained every year with the hopes of inducing some small impulse of gratitude where there is only impatience to get back to the games on television and shared amazement at the fact that Christmas decorations and music have already appeared in the shopping mall. How can we rejoice at gathering in the sheaves when we have never held a pungent bundle of grain in our arms nor swam with the dying grasshoppers in the oats? You can look in vain through our modern hymnals for the old gospel song, 'Bringing in the Sheaves.' But I know the chorus by heart.

We sang slowly and softly, 'Sowing in the morning, sowing seeds of kindness/ Sowing in the noontide and the dewy eve/ Waiting for the harvest, and the time of reaping/We shall come rejoicing, bringing in the sheaves." I could hardly wait for the chorus, which we sang at the top of our voices, "*Bringing in the sheaves, bringing in the sheaves/ We shall come rejoicing, bringing in the sheaves/ Bringing in the sheaves, bringing in the sheaves/ We shall come rejoicing, bringing in the sheaves.*"

Today, the oats are still harvested on the same land on which I struggled as a young boy to wrestle the bundles into the semblance of a standing shock. But now the harvester is a self-propelled monster of its own making, the operator riding in an air conditioned cab, with the roar of the machine muted and no dust to creep under a hot collar, gliding through the still-sanding grain faster than a man can walk. The bin of threshed oats is transferred by an auger into a large truck running alongside, to be driven to a nearby grain elevator in town where it is dumped by a hydraulic lift and the check deposited directly into a bank account, waiting to be spent on a down payment on another quarter-section of land, or a new and larger harvester. "Looks like you had a good crop this year, Bill," I heard one farmer say to another. "Yep," he replied, "but unfortunately it was all spent before I harvested it."

Inexpressible Gratitude

This is not going to be easy. Writing about gratitude, I mean. I once thought that gratitude was one thing and hope was another. But then I discovered that those who felt the deepest gratitude were those who had harvested something hoped for. To reap what another has sown is to live by another's hope. If this is done knowingly it is close to the sin of thievery; if done unknowingly it becomes the sin of ingratitude. But ingratitude is not a decision we make. It is not as though I am aware that I owe someone a response and a word of thanks, but I am just not going to do it. It is not as though I feel gratitude and thankfulness but for some obstinate reason refuse to express it.

No, it is more likely that ingratitude is due to being stuck in a stage of immaturity where my sense of entitlement becomes an insatiable demand that my needs are the measure of a just world. Or it could be that the intimacy and familiarity of shared life and love produces a debt too profound to pay.

Recently I preached a sermon during the thanksgiving season in which I called to mind the realization of how much my mother and father sacrificed and gave to me out of sheer love. It was unconditional on their part. That is why it was so easy to accept. Unconditional love requires no payment in kind. That is why it can be accepted so freely and also why, at the same time, it calls for such profound gratitude. I recalled that during the time that my parents were still alive, not once did I summon up the courage to look them straight in the eye and say, "Mother, I now realize what you have given me through your own love from the time I was a small child; I want you to know how grateful I am." Never did I look into my father's face and say, "Dad, I am who I am because of you. I thank you for giving me all that you have through the years."

It's too late now, of course. It is always too late with regard to unconditional love. But now I am fully aware of what my parents have given to me. I am no longer a child caught in the paralysis of immaturity, living off the hope of others in the complacency of ingratitude. Suppose that I now had the chance. With the full awareness and sense of propriety that comes with maturity (assuming that this is the case!), could I now look my mother in the eye and express my gratitude to her? When I create that scenario in my mind, I know immediately that I could not do it. I can not think of the words that would carry the weight of that enormous gratitude without in the very speaking them, know instantly that they were trite and trivial.

I remember Dietrich Bonhoeffer writing about the difference between the ultimate and the penultimate, the last word and the next to the last. I wrote of this earlier in Chapter Eight. He used an example based on the role of a pastor in calling on a person who is in deep grief. "Why is it," he asks, "that precisely in thoroughly grave situations, for instance when I am with someone who has suffered a bereavement, I often decide to adopt a 'penultimate' attitude, particularly when I am dealing with Christians, remaining silent as a sign that I share in the bereaved man's helplessness in the face of such a grievous event, and not speaking the biblical words of comfort which are, in fact, known to me and available to me. Why am I often unable to open my mouth, when I ought to give expression to the ultimate? And why, instead do I decide on an expression of thoroughly penultimate human solidarity? Is it from mistrust of the power of the ultimate word? Is it from fear of men? Or is there some good positive reason for such an attitude, namely, that my knowledge of the word, my having it at my finger-tips, in other words my being, so to speak, spiritually master of the situation, bears only the appearance of the ultimate, but is in reality something entirely penultimate? Does not one in some cases, by remaining deliberately in the penultimate, perhaps point all the more genuinely to the ultimate, which God will speak in His own time (though indeed even then through a human mouth)?"

I quote this in full because I have a sense that he is pointing us to a profound truth, not merely about the art of pastoral care, but the very structure of human social relationships. In fact, he goes on to suggest just that. "What we have said about this particular case applies in countless instances to the daily life of Christians together, and to the whole activity of the Christian preacher with his flock."

The penultimate in this sense refers to our present time-bound existence where we struggle to reveal our deepest thoughts and desires to each other across the space that unites us but also divides us. The Apostle Paul spoke of the penultimate when he wrote: "For now we see in a mirror, dimly, then we will see face to face. Now I know only in part; then I will know fully, even as I have been fully known" (1 Cor. 13:12). We thus have this hope of being able to communicate and share fully and freely what we now express partially and even conceal for the sake of preserving love from being merely words. This is how gratitude lives with hope.

Is then gratitude sometimes so profound that it cannot be authentically spoken in the penultimate? I can and did, say 'thank you' to my mother for a Christmas present, but never for giving birth to me and feeding me at her breast in order that I might live. Would not 'thank you' for such a profound gift of life be utterly superficial, trivial and thus even inappropriate? But then how does one express gratitude to God for his unconditional love and gracious gift of salvation life? Paul does say, "Thanks be to God for his indescribable gift" (2 Cor 9:15)! But even this is in the third person, and not addressed directly to God.

I think that I can understand why some feel that only when they experience the so-called 'gift of tongues,' uttering sounds that are not intelligible words as an expression of worship, do they break out of the 'silence of the penultimate' in order to communicate directly with God. But if I understand Bonhoeffer, even here one moves out of the ordinary 'solidarity' that we experience with God's presence into the extraordinary as only an occasional utterance of what is meant to be a continuous, though unspoken, gratitude. In this case, the ordinary is ruptured by the extraordinary; and how do you repair it once it is torn?

When I imagine having such a moment with my father in which I break through this invisible, but almost tangible curtain that enables us to be present to one another, to overwhelm him with my expressions of gratitude, what is left? What do we do next? How does one get back smoothly and safely into the penultimate when the ultimate has been spoken? I have somewhat the same feeling with regard to expressing gratitude to God. If gratitude is an everyday expression of the penultimate, the extraordinary language of worship may not be a sign of God's presence, but rather of his absence. It is easier to be caught up in rapturous praise of God when he is not looking. Face to face with Jesus I don't think that I would want to be so overcome that I enjoy a private time of worship while he waits to have a conversation with me. I will let him be the first one to speak in an unknown tongue. I think that gratitude can be sensed before it is sung.

I think that this is why Bonhoeffer warned us that the penultimate has its own integrity and why even gratitude, especially gratitude, is best a shared experience in the ordinary living of our lives rather than depending upon extraordinary means of 'breaking that silence.' Theologian Paul Tillich was once quoted as saying, "The concept of God's extraordinary presence in our lives entails also the concept of his ordinary absence." In other words, if the only time we recognize God's presence is through some supernatural intervention, we are really assuming his absence in all the other times.

This of course does not rule out occasional and extraordinary celebrations in the midst of the penultimate. We celebrated my mother's birthday and gave her a present only once a year, but expressed our gratitude for her presence in our lives by 'being present' every day of the year. The grace of gratitude is an everyday expression of love that, in being unspoken and often invisible, makes its occasional celebration authentic and joyful. There is then a place for celebration in worship, but even that is part of the penultimate. There is a special thanksgiving that belongs to the gathering of the harvest that only has merit because it is a grace that is practiced in receiving each day as the gift of the Creator.

The Practice of Gratitude

Gratitude must be practiced; it is not a natural instinct. We were taught by our parents to pause before eating and give thanks to God. Ingratitude is a natural instinct; every infant demonstrates that. Whether or not one attributes ingratitude to what theologians call 'original sin,' does not matter to parents. Ingratitude can be tolerated and excused for those who are immature. But there comes a point when there is no excuse. The Apostle Paul warns of the dire consequences when humanity assumes the right to their own life rather than as a gift of the Creator. To live without gratitude is to live without God. We all should know better, says Paul. "So they are without excuse; for though they knew God, they did not honor him as God or give thanks to him, but became futile in their thinking, and their senseless minds were darkened" (Rom 1:21).

This is why gratitude is not just one of the fruits of the Spirit, like generosity, gentleness, joy or peace (Gal 5:23). Nor is ingratitude listed as one of the 'works of the flesh,' like strife, envy, jealousy and anger (Gal 5:19-20). Ingratitude is not a character fault nor is it merely a personality trait. Ingratitude is in fact a form of rebellion; it is not just a passive temperament or lack of social grace. Every parent knows that behind the stubborn refusal of a child to acknowledge with gratitude its dependence upon others for its own existence is an act of rebellion manifested by fits of anger and outrage at not getting its own way. Nor can a child be 'trained' to overcome this habit of ingratitude through a series of rewards and punishment. Behavior modification is only that, a modification of behavior rather than the acquisition of a grace-filled life. Ingratitude is a deep fault with respect to being and relating to others as personal being. It is rebellion against the demand to be personal, that is, to exist in a structure of dependence upon others for one's own being.

The original context of a person's life is one of relationship, ordinarily that of a parent or caretaker who draws the infant into a relation through motives of love and care. This is intended to produce reciprocity in the child so that 'being in relation' is not merely conforming to rules or regulations (behavior) but responding to the intentionality of the caregiver in personal, relational terms. Here the response is not first of all intentional on the part of the child, but is produced through the feelings that the child has for the caregiver. These feelings are themselves either positive or negative. If they are positive, they are the early stages of gratitude that overcomes the negative feelings of resistance based on getting power through self-control. The child then is empowered by the intentional love of the other to respond; the positive response is gratitude expressed through relation to the other.

This is the 'starting point' of gratitude as the core of personal being. John Macmurray, a Scottish philosopher with whom I met during my time of study in Scotland, says of this original starting point. "It is not left behind as the child grows up. It remains the ground pattern of all personal motivation at every stage of development." The point of maturity in this developmental process, says Macmurray, "is not independence, but a mutual interdependence of equals." Gratitude then is an orientation of the self towards another. This orientation is always subject to the limitations of the availability of the other, either due to the fact that those upon whom we are dependent for mutual care and support fail or to the fact that relationship itself is a promise that can only be fulfilled beyond this temporal life. Gratitude thus, is the single ingredient of life that keeps hope alive.

Gratitude is as Gratitude Does

This is a paraphrase of the saying that Forrest Gump, in the movie by this name, attributed to his mother, "Stupid is as stupid does." Attempts to define gratitude as an abstract noun fail. Gratitude is a relational quality; being in relationship is itself a gift. Being there in the relation is to receive the gift and is a positive motive expressed toward the other as the one who makes the relation possible. This positive motive, as I wrote above, is not yet an intention for the infant, but when it becomes intentional this original motive that may at first be only a feeling, produces a mutuality of unconditional trust and love. Gratitude is a form of mutuality where there is unconditional love. And God is love.

Gratitude as an expression of our relation to God is thus not something that we 'owe' God nor something that we give to God, leaving us free to be 'ourselves.' Rather, being in relation to God is more like friendship than being a disciple. Jesus told his disciples that he would call them 'his friends' because he had shared with them everything that he had heard from the Father (John 15:15). In our efforts to disciple new believers, we may have missed the point. To be a disciple is to undertake a calling to follow Christ, or to serve Christ by carrying our his mission in the world. But I have known some who have been 'discipled' in this manner to end up becoming frustrated, burned out, and yes, ungrateful! Some may conclude the implication that being a disciple is a way of earning a reward, or gaining some merit. And there are scriptural texts that do speak of rewards for our service in Christ. But if one serves in order to gain a reward then one can hardly be grateful for the reward, for a reward is earned, not a gift. If one feels that the reward is not sufficient or is delayed, then one begins to experience ingratitude. In the parable of the prodigal son, the elder brother becomes angry and resentful when the father receives the son back without a penalty or punishment. The father responds, "Son, you are always with me, and all that is mine is yours" (Luke 15:31). The elder son cannot enter into the thanksgiving celebration for his brother; he has no gratitude for his brother's return because he is living with ingratitude.

Gratitude was a year-round way of living for my father. While he could permit himself to celebrate some at harvest time, he did not need a good harvest to thank God. Nor did he have to wait for the Thanksgiving season to sing his gratitude.

We Give thee but thine own, What e're the gift may be;
All that we have is Thine alone, A Trust, O Lord, from Thee.

Chapter 12 - Reinvesting

Suffering a Loss Without Losing Hope

In all the years growing up on the farm there was only one in which there was no harvest. The drought of 1932 hit the mid-west farming community where we lived with a vengeance. The seed was planted in dry soil with hope of rain. It never came. Instead, the hot winds came and along with it the blowing dust that created drifts along the fence rows and sifted through cracks in the windows leaving a sooty film on everything inside. The reaper was not used that fall. Instead, weeds that survived along the roads and stunted grain that never reached maturity were mowed and stored as hay to feed the cows. What little grain remained from the previous year was saved as seed for the following spring.

I remember my mother asking my father at the supper table that fall, "Do we have enough to get through the winter?" He answered, "Yes, and a little bit more. We will just have to tighten our belts and wait until next year."

I have heard that expressions many times, and never quite understood its source. My guess is that scarcity of food causes one to loose weight and one has to 'tighten' the belt a notch or two to keep the trousers from falling down. We did make it through, and there was no weeping, no bitter complaining. Suffering even a devastating loss does not, need not, cause the death of hope. A loss can break your heart, but that is what hope risks.

We can only have strong feelings for that which has the capacity to break our hearts. We can only mend a broken heart by sowing the seeds for a future harvest. My father loved the soil and the seed more than the harvest! This is the lesson hope teaches us. This is why the security of the soul for a farmer better not rest solely on the prospect of a harvest!

Life is best lived from one sowing to another, not one harvest to another. This I discovered from living dependent upon the cycle of nature, living between the sowing and the reaping. The good harvest is a time of rejoicing and thanksgiving at life's bounty. But those who live by the harvest, die by the harvest. If harvest is all that stirs the heart, what is left when the harvest fails?

Life is a venture where good fortune is desired and misfortune is feared. If we wish to pay the premium, we can insure against some of life's misfortunes which have a material or financial impact. Insurance however, does not prevent misfortune, it only serves to compensate for the loss caused by misfortune. Some farmers pay an annual premium for hail insurance on their crops. But that is only one of the risks that can ruin a good harvest. One cannot insure against every calamity which can strike down a good harvest. Too much rain at the wrong time, extended drought, plant disease, or an early frost, are just some of the many hazards of nature that can become personal misfortune when one's hopes are invested in the harvest.

The Tragic Dimension of Hope

There is something intrinsically tragic when it comes to hope. When one dares to hope within a finite world and when what one hopes for suffers failure and loss, hope must be prepared to embrace the tragic. Hope creates possibilities beyond what can be realized and desires which can never be fulfilled on the stage of life. The curtain always falls on this stage at the end, where the dreams we dream and the longings we feel are left hanging in the empty space long after the applause has died away. Theologian Wendy Farley says, "Created perfection is fragile, tragically structured. The tragic structure of finitude and the human capacity for deception and cruelty together account for the possibility and actuality of suffering and evil."

Most people do not like the word 'tragic.' They want to erase it from the vocabulary of hope as though denying its existence as part of the good world they can eliminate its possibility from the real world. They can accept the tragic as due to sin, but not as a reality of hope. The passion of hope with its capacity to embrace the tragic is what gives faith its enduring power. I suffer for those who dare not hope for fear of having to let go, in time at least, of that for which one hopes. Embracing the tragic element imbedded in hope at the beginning is not to lose hope but to have hope that endures loss.

The American poet, Ridgely Torrence, captures in sparse words the mingling of the tragic with the harvest of hope.

> I heard an old farm-wife,
> Selling some barley,
> Mingle her life with life

And the name "Charley."

Saying: "The crop's all in,
We're about through now;
Long nights will soon begin,
We're just us two now.

"Twelve bushel at sixty cents,
It's all I carried—
He sickened making fence;
He was to be married—

"It feels like frost was near—
His hair was curly,
The spring was late that year,
But the harvest was early."

Each word carries more pain than language was meant to bear. Only the poet dares to strike this chord. For most of us, a tragic loss and a promising harvest are separate strings on the instrument called life, not meant to be struck together. But hope when played as a single note, can become shrill and even unpleasant when played in the presence of an unbearable loss. Those who dare to hope are destined to suffer. This can be devastating for one who hopes too early and for too much. We turn from the poet to the novelist for our next lesson in hope.

In his novel, *Of Human Bondage*, Somerset Maugham recounts an incident from childhood, slightly fictionalized from which his faith never recovered. The main character, Philip, has just discovered the verse in the gospel of Mark which says, "Whatever you ask for in prayer, believe that you have received it, and it will be yours" (11:24).

He thinks immediately of his clubfoot.

He would be able to play football. His heart leaped as he saw himself running faster than any of the other boys. At the end of Easter term there were the sports, and he would be able to go in for the races; he rather fancied himself over the hurdles. It would be splendid to be like everyone else, not to be stared at curiously by new boys who did not know about his deformity, nor at the baths in summer to need incredible precautions, while he was undressing, before he could hide his foot in the water.

He prayed with all the power in his soul. No doubts assailed him. He was confident in the Word of God. And the night before he was to go back to school he went up to bed tremulous with excitement. There was snow on the ground, and Aunt Louisa had allowed herself the unaccustomed luxury of a fire in her bedroom, but in Philip's little room it was so cold that his fingers were numb, and he had great difficulty undoing his collar. His teeth chattered. The idea came to him that he must do something more unusual to attract the attention of God, and he turned back the rug which was in front of his bed so that he could kneel on the bare boards, and then it struck him that his nightshirt was a softness that might displease his Maker, so he took it off and said his prayers naked. When he got into bed he was so cold that for some time he could not sleep, but when he did, it was so soundly that Mary Ann had to shake him when she brought his hot water next morning.

She talked to him while she drew the curtains, but he did not answer; he had remembered at once that this was the morning of the miracle. His heart was filled with joy and gratitude. His first instinct was to put down his hand and feel the foot which was whole now, but to do this seemed to doubt the goodness of God. He knew that his foot was well. But at last he made up his mind, and with the toes of his right foot he just touched his left. Then he passed his hand over it. He limped downstairs just as Mary Ann was going into the dining room for prayers, and then he sat down to breakfast. 'You're very quiet this morning, Philip,' said Aunt Louisa presently.

When hope is embraced where faith has not yet matured, the damage can be permanent. There is a childish hope that doesn't count. I remember hoping for things that were merely objects of pleasure. Failure to receive them resulted in momentary disappointment but not deep grief. My attachments were passionate but superficial. Somewhere this changed. Perhaps it was what the Apostle Paul meant when he said, "When I was a child, I spoke like a child, I thought like a child, I reasoned like a child; when I became an adult I put away childish ways" (1 Cor 13:11). There are texts of Scripture, such as the one from Mark discovered by Philip in Maugham's story that should be marked, 'Keep Out of the Hands of Children!' Hope is dangerous when it is placed in the hands of children who have not yet learned to strike the chord that includes the tragic.

Even the disciples of Jesus, after spending three years with Jesus, lost their hope and faith when confronted by his tragic death on the cross. When questioned by Jesus after his resurrection as to why they were so sad, two of his disciples, not recognizing him said, "We had hoped that he was the one to redeem Israel" (Luke 24:21). It was their loss of hope that blinded them to the reality of his presence and turned them back to a life of despair. They were the fortunate ones. Judas not only turned against Jesus and betrayed him when he saw his hope for a Messiah crushed by a crucifixion, but took his own life in despair and remorse. Hope can be dangerous when put in the hands of those who lack the maturity to embrace the tragic.

When we venture our life in relationships and undertake commitments where it is possible to lose what we love the most, we can experience a loss for which there is no insurance or means for compensation. A loss of that which we have loved and in which we have made investments of passion and patience is often heartbreaking. There is something redemptive about hope, however; hope is itself the medicine for a heart broken by hope.

Herein lies a strange but compelling paradox. When we fail to realize that for which we hope, we experience that as loss of hope. "I've lost hope," we often say when some goal or project becomes impossible. But what we have lost is not hope, but rather that on which we have pinned our hope. Hope survives when it is reinvested. When we feel that we have lost hope, we have to grieve the loss while reinvesting hope.

Reinvesting Hope After a Loss

All losses need to be grieved, no matter how trivial they may seem to others. Each person's loss is greater than that of others. For losses are personally weighted not progressively graded. It is the experience of divine grace, often mediated through the care and love others, that finally enables us to recover from loss. Grief is the process of reaching that grace. The process of grieving a loss is paradoxical in its intention. Through grief one seeks to heal the pain of loss, let go of what can no longer be kept, and face the reality of living with only a memory of what once was. The lovely poem by Lisel Mueller, "In Passing," captures this thought exquisitely:

> How swiftly the strained honey
> of afternoon light
> flows into darkness
> and the closed bud shrugs off
> its special mystery
> in order to break into blossom:
> as if what exists, exists
> so that it can be lost
> and become precious.

When we are caught in the throes of grieving a loss, it is sometimes hard to grow out of the grief. The intense feeling of grief can sometime be the only way to remain connected to what has been lost. When this happens we get stuck in the loss cycle of recovery, unable to move on to a new life of hope. Grief becomes a ritual of attachment to what no longer exists, hindering our growth toward the grace of recovery.

Just the opposite can happen as well. The feeling of grief can be so great that it becomes repressed and a 'will to survive' takes over. 'I'm a survivor,' some like to say, as if to assure themselves that, while they have suffered loss, the game of life is not over. Grieving through to grace goes beyond survival to the recovery of the self's capacity to reinvest hope. Grace is growth and growth moves through phases, each adding strength to hope and faith. Grace empowers the self, enabling it to retain the memory of what was lost while letting go of the object that was lost.

Because grace is creative it has its source in a Creator God. Because grace is restorative it has its power in a Redeemer God. Because grace is inspiring it communicates its life through the Spirit of God. Through grief we apprehend the grace of God, and by the grace of God we recover the courage to reinvest hope when hope has failed.

Grieving through to grace opens up the vault where grief stores its treasures and ritually mourns its losses. When the golden grain we have harvested, sometimes prematurely, from the first sowing of love becomes new seed for sowing, we have recovered hope. The seeds which we now sow are those which we have reaped from the sorrow and tragedy of earlier losses. This is what the cycle of life teaches us. Those who demonstrate the unusual power to strike back when misfortune strikes have learned to exercise the power of hope. They save some seed from every harvest to sow in the fields savaged by the cruel storms of life. These people are not exceptional saints, they are ordinary sowers empowered by grace.

When we envision the planting of new seeds we look past the ruins of a failed harvest with hope toward the coming spring, a time of growth and renewal. Preparing for a harvest takes only a few days, or even hours. Preparing to sow new seeds requires months of waiting through the long winter, anticipating the warm spring sun and the stirring of the soil. Sowing has to do with preparing the seed, preparing the soil, and attending the new growth. All of this is the way that we reinvest hope.

At the same time, it is necessary to make emotional investments in order to plant the seed of love in the soil of life. The risk of failure is no reason not to go forth and plant. "In the morning sow your seed, and at evening do not let your hands be idle; for you do not know which will prosper, this or that, or whether both alike will be good" (Ecclesiastes 11:6).

The recovery of hope includes an expansion of the self, allowing time for the fragments of the self to find a place in the nourishing soil of the human family. Recovery begins with the discovery that what appeared to be a gaping hole in the seamless robe of our fragile happiness is the edge of darkness caused by the setting of the sun. Awakening in the midst of the 'dead of night,' where the soul lies still and the heart is silent, there is the rising of the moon, now in the luminous phase of fullness. At last comes the time for sowing, even a second or third time, as Anne Morrow Lindberg poetically puts it, after losing her own son in a tragic kidnapping.

> There is no harvest for the heart alone;
> The seed of love must be
> Eternally Resown.

There is a burden that hope must bear. There is a burden to hope that tears away at the spirit when failure occurs. "Hope deferred makes the heart sick," the proverb reminds us (Prov 13:12). The burden of hope is the weakness of the seed and our own helplessness to care for it in the face of the unpredictable storms of life. Without rain the seed will not grow. But with every rain cloud there looms the possibility of a ravaging and cruel storm. Not every rain will produce a flood, nor will every cloud produce some rain. Not every sickness leads to a death, but death does occur, senseless and outrageous to the human spirit. Hope is the burden that one must bear to live by faith and the promise of God. The burden of hope is the anguish over what has already been lost. Hope always emerges out of the ruins of some failed dream, some unfulfilled desire, some loss that must be grieved.

Those who have the courage and faith to bear forth the seed, as the Psalmist reminds us, also bear the burden of the seed.

> He surely toils along weeping,
> carrying the burden of seed;
> he surely comes in with rejoicing,
> carrying his sheaves.
> (Psalm 126, literal translation of the Hebrew)

Hope was first expressed in the Bible following the first murder. Eve was the mother of two sons, Cain and Abel. When Cain killed Abel, we read, "Adam knew his wife again, and she bore a son and named him Seth, for she said, 'God has appointed for me another child instead of Abel, because Cain killed him'" (Gen. 4:25). I can hear her whisper to herself, "Will Cain slay him? Will I lose this son too?"

There are those who would not have risked another child, another tragic loss. There are those who prefer never to try again rather than to suffer the anguish of bearing hope. Having lost one child, can one bear the burden of hope and risk another one? Will the burden of anguish and responsibility be too much? How will one survive through the inevitable childhood sicknesses that follow the birth of every child, when sickness has already produced one death? Not all jealousy and hatred leads to murder. But murders and violence do occur. Eve has chosen to have another child. There will be jealousy and anger again, can one bear the burden of helplessness in the face of such uncertainty? Having been betrayed once, will one dare to trust again? Not every plot that develops in human relationships becomes a betrayal. But is there any real relationship without the sub-plots which have the power to destroy what love has created? No, but that is the role of hope. Even when faith falters hope comes to the rescue. When my father lost a harvest he did not lose faith because he had reserved a small portion of last year's harvest as seed for the next year. When he told my mother, "We have enough and a little bit more," the seed was 'enough' and the 'little bit more' was hope. Somewhere deep down in every soul crushed by failure and stricken with loss there is a longing to reinvest in hope of another harvest.

The seed of hope is longing and longing is a renewable quality of the human spirit. At the very end with the wood for his cross already cut, Jesus gathered his disciples and told them, "I have been very eager to eat this Passover meal with you before my suffering begins" (Luke 22:15 NLT). "Come before winter," Paul wrote to his friend Timothy from prison (2 Tim 4:21). We carry the longing for spring into every winter. This is what keeps hope alive.

Part Four

WINTER

The Vision of Hope

Brogan
January 15, 1991

Our children sow their precious seed,
in flesh covered soil, watered by tears;
a child is born, by an ancient creed,
and gives his youth to an old man's years.
         I am Springtime's Child.

The wind bends low the golden grain,
and blends the scent of air and earth;
in swirling clouds and smell of rain,
a sensuous womb for an infant's birth.
         I am Summer's Child.

A harvest moon hallows the sky,
bathing wounded earth with mystical art;
in the lonely night the wild geese cry,
singing siren's song in a small boy's heart.
         I am Autumn's Child.

As drifting snow quilts the frozen land,
in a storied stable, a quiet diversion;
on Christmas eve the cows all stand,
birthing Christ again in a young man's vision.
         I am Winter's Child.

For you, my son, I've lived the seasons,
in you, my child, my spirit grows;
in your heart are all the reasons,
why God is love and surely knows
                    that you are Brogan!
                                    RSA

Chapter 13 - Repairing

Putting Everything Back in Working Order

Some of the most important work to be done is when there is no work to be done. This apparently paradoxical statement was put in my mind by my father's response to my question as to why he insisted that we get out the farm implements and the harness for the horses after the harvest was in and the fall field-work was done. "Why are we doing this now," I asked? "We won't need to use this until next year."

With patience seasoned through the endurance of a small boy's attempts to get out of all unnecessary work, he replied, "We don't put anything away until it is back in good working order," and then added, "It is easier to fix something when we aren't using it."

With that we repaired and oiled the heavy leather harness for each of the six horses, replaced worn gears with new ones on the mower and reaper, sharpened plow shares and took pieces of machinery that had been wired together in the field to the local blacksmith to be welded. These were evidences of break-downs during planting and harvest and signs of some to come unless repairs were made. Today, my nephew operates a farm of several thousand acres and runs a harvesting combine that costs upwards of $200,000. It has dozens of belts and probably a thousand moving parts, not to mention more sophisticated computer equipment than I use in writing these pages. Each fall he drives it into the local implement dealer to have it completely serviced at a cost of at least $10,000 in anticipation of having it in good working order for next year's crop that may or not require its use, depending upon the weather. This is the work that hope requires in order that hope may do its work. I have discovered that this maxim is not only conventional wisdom for those who invest their work in the soil but also for those who invest their soul in their work.

The seasons no longer order my life by the rhythm of preparing, sowing, reaping and resting. Nor do they for most of us; 24/7 has become more than shorthand for 'all day/everyday.' It is a mantra for a more efficient life often at the cost of a more effective one. The days flow into weeks, the weeks into months and a new year eclipses an old year with only a passing glance. My latest automobile requires service every 15,000 miles and that only occurs once every two years. I take daily medication to lower blood pressure so that I need not take time to 'smell the flowers' and give my body a chance to discharge unhealthy tension by its own rhythm. I only call a repair-man after something is broken. Meanwhile, I hope nothing, including my own body, breaks down.

Some of the most important work to be done is when there is no work to be done. Don't put anything away until it is put back in good working order. What if I applied this to my own life and made it a rule to keep before going to bed at night? Attempting to fall asleep while still doing repair work can wreak havoc with a good night's rest!

Let's find a way to apply this bit of conventional farm-life wisdom to our reflections on the seasons of hope.

We humans experience anxiety and stress that animals seem not to have. When I fed my cows the last bale of hay it satisfied their hunger and gave them 'cud to chew' and contentment on their faces. I was aware however, that there was no more hay for the next feeding. I carried that knowledge to bed and the stress of having to think of ways to purchase some for the next day. Of course, I had anticipated that, and suffered several sleepless nights of stress, for I had the foresight to count the bales in order to prevent the distressing situation of running out of hay! This is both the blessing and curse of awareness, and thus of hope. As the author of the book of Ecclesiastes reminds us, God has "planted eternity in the human heart, but even so, people cannot see the whole scope of God's work from beginning to end" (Ecc 3:11 NLT).

This is why hope can lead to anxiety and even induce stress. To hope for that which we cannot determine or produce by our own effort adds anxiety to the 'daily care' that is required of us in order to meet our needs and accomplish our tasks. This is why Jesus said, "So don't worry about tomorrow, for tomorrow will bring its own worries. Today's trouble is enough for today" (Mt 6:34 NLT). Fine, but add future hope to daily care and it is enough to cause a break-down! This is why hope can cause stress. And stress is often attributed to a break-down, whether emotionally or physically. So what is the solution?

Stress itself is not the problem, I am told. Stress is normal. In fact some degree of stress is necessary. Without stress caused by the regular and rhythmic contraction of a heart muscle, blood would not be forced through the arteries to the extremities of the body. Creativity requires the stress of facing an empty canvas for the artist and an empty page for the writer. The problem is not stress but 'distress.' What otherwise would be creative, invigorating and nourishing stress as a positive force in our lives, can become 'anxious stress' or distress.

For Jesus, it was not the daily stress of ministry, healing, and casting out of demons that required him to 'pause for repair.' It was the stress of leaving so many unhealed. It was not the stress of feeding 5,000 that burdened him, but the distress of the thousands who went to bed hungry that very night. The daily work of his ministry, he explained was really the work of the Father through him (John 4:34). What caused him distress was not the work of the Father that required his devotion and duty, but the larger sphere of humanity where the Father was not working. He could heal the man who had lain paralyzed for 38 years, but had to leave many others lying there in their infirmity (John 5). He could raise Lazarus from the grave, acknowledging that it was really the work and for the glory of the Father while others were left in the tomb (John 11). What answer did he have for the relatives of those who were not raised? We can easily focus on the miracles of healing the one blind man (John 9) without realizing that Jesus knew that hundreds of other blind persons heard about that and remained blind. In the face of so much distress, how could Jesus retain his composure if not also his sanity?

When stress becomes distress, compassion has turned into compulsion. The compassion of Jesus for those who suffered, whether mentally, socially, or physically is so well known that the word is virtually a synonym for his character. His tears at the tomb of Lazarus are not the only ones that he shed. On his last trip to Jerusalem Luke tells us that as he drew near and saw the city he "wept over it" (Luke 19:41). If Jesus was constantly moved with compassion at the plight of others, how did he keep that compassion from becoming a compulsion to stop everything else and allow the needs of those around him to determine his agenda? Why did not the 'work of ministry' cause him to 'burn out' as it has with so many who undertake this calling? How could he in good conscience turn away from the hundreds who were suffering all about him and minister to the few that were brought to him?

The gospels speak of Jesus rising early in the morning to pray, and even spending the entire night in prayer (Mark 1:35; Luke 6:12). We are not told specifically what he did during these hours nor what he prayed for. We can only speculate. I think that these were times in which he did his repair work. This is the important work to be done when there is no

work to be done. It was during these times, I think, that he discussed with
the Father, 'what is mine and what is yours' with regard to the responsibilities confronting him each day. Here it was that he could work out
with the father 'what can be done tomorrow and what can wait for the
future.' It was during these hours that he could release his compassion
from becoming a compulsion and renegotiate as it were, his contract with
the Father with regard to priorities and performance. If compassion was
his contact with the world, his contract was to do the will of his Father
who sent him (John 4:34). What might appear to be an aimless and itiner-
ant wandering from one end of the county to another, and from mingling
with the multitudes to a retreat into solitude, was the way in which Jesus
honed his instincts to interpret events as they related to his destiny. This is
'seasonal repair work' plotted in the daily diary of an emerging Messiah.
And this is our clue as to how we can keep hope on the horizon while
living each day to its fullest.

Keeping Our Lives in Working Order

The season of repairing with regard to hope is not an event on our
calendar, it is a rhythm of renewal and restoration that has its own pace
and place. The work that hope does when it is not working is neither a
temporary spiritual retreat from a daily secular occupation nor a passive
withdrawal from activity into monastic meditation. Repairing is necessary
work, indeed it may be the most important work of all for it is a way of
restoring our life to working order. Based on my portrayal of the routine
of repair that may well have kept Jesus from compulsive compassion that
leads to spiritual exhaustion, here are some suggestions for taking the exit
ramp and heading for the repair shop.

Renegotiating Our Contract With Life

In assuming responsibility for our own lives, at whatever point in the
transition from childhood to adulthood, there is an implied contract in
which we assume certain responsibilities with the promise of a reward or
benefit. This has to do with hope in both the temporal and eternal sphere.
If we hope for some degree of independent living we take over the control
of our lives from others and release them from responsibility to provide
for us, in that area at least. Assuming control over our own lives however, while that may yield benefits that otherwise would be unattainable
is in effect, a 'work contract' in which we have pledged our emotional,
mental, physical and spiritual resources. Even if we were to call this a
matter of 'faith rather than works,' faith apart from works is dead, says
James (James 2:20). This does not refer to 'religious work' as an attempt

to earn righteousness, but the 'outworking' of faith in which we reap the fruit of faith (Col. 1:10). What constitutes repair is not cessation of work in order that what we hope for might just 'drop in our lap.' Rather the work itself needs to be repaired. In this case the work I am speaking of is embedded in the implied contract by which we have assumed control in order to reap some benefit.

In order to gain the greatest benefit of hope we often bind ourselves to the highest degree of control, assuming that if we have control we have a grasp on what we hope for. Jesus assumed just the opposite. When he felt constrained by compassion to meet the needs of the entire world of suffering humanity by his own efforts, he released himself from that which he could not control. He stood within arms-reach of the man born blind from birth and knew instinctively that it was his responsibility to reach out and touch him and heal him (John 9). Beyond that he took no control over the hundreds of other blind persons and released himself from the responsibility to hunt them down and heal them in order to gain his Father's approval. When told by the sisters of Lazarus that their brother, 'whom he loved' was sick and dying, Jesus remained where he was until he felt sent by the Father to raise him from the dead. I would have dropped everything and immediately run to heal him allowing my compassion to become a compulsion to help. But Jesus had done his repair work. He too felt the constraint of compassion and the urge to meet every need in order to fulfill his mission. But his mission, as he discovered over and over again in the repair shop, was not to save the world by himself but to serve the Father who had sent him into the world. Thus the will of the Father was more than an ethical concern of Jesus to do the right thing, it was his *only* concern as the Son of the Father.

"Purity of Heart is to Do One Thing," wrote the Danish theologian Søren Kierkegaard. Never mind trying to determine what the one thing is ahead of time, he wrote, it is not a matter of ethics but of conformity to God. When there is finally only *one thing* to do that demands all of our heart, then that is the right thing. We are released from all of the other things that may lay a claim to our responsibility to God. In the parable of the good Samaritan (Luke 10), the Samaritan came within eyesight of the wounded man by the road and immediately knew that this was the 'one thing' that was demanded of him in order to be a good neighbor. He was not out searching for victims in order to fulfill his quota for the day. While ministering to that one he released himself from the ethical and spiritual responsibility to respond to others in that moment. When we make the concerns of others a contract that binds us to their needs we are assuming responsibilities over which we have no control. For us at least (I am not sure about Jesus) this is why we need to take hope to the repair shop frequently and work over our contract with God and our life. Compulsive work may be the unconscious and psychological cause of legalism, attempting to gain approval (hope) through our own efforts. What exactly is the repair that needs to be done while hope is not working?

Realigning our Life with the Kingdom of God

Jesus warned that his followers were not to be like the Gentiles but rather to "Seek first the Kingdom of God" (Mt 6:31-33). The Kingdom of God includes 'all things' but all things do not necessarily include the Kingdom of God. The Gentiles were not bad people, they were just out of alignment. It is a rule of thumb that when any moving part in a machine goes out of alignment, the machine will sooner or later self-destruct. If we shift the focus to hope, the metaphor still applies.

Hope is the lodestar that keeps faith on course. Faith is the intentionality that raises the sail in hopes of catching a friendly breeze bringing us at last to the safe harbor of our desires and dreams. Without hope, faith is susceptible to the fickle winds of fortune and fate. The Apostle Paul assures us that "hope does not disappoint us, because God's love has been poured into our hearts through the Holy Spirit that has been given to us" (Rom 5:5). But this assumes that we have our priorities in life aligned with the Kingdom of God. The problem with the Gentiles, as Jesus referred to them, was that their alignment was on the things that they needed for daily life without regard for the one thing that they needed for eternal life.

When Jesus said, "Truly I tell you, unless you change and become like children, you will never enter the kingdom of Heaven" (Mt 18:3), he implied that there is some essential goodness which the child possesses and which needs to be cared for. When Jesus exhorted us to "receive the kingdom of God as a little child," it means that we re-discover the longing which opens us up to God's love and the fulfillment of the self in another. It may well be that Jesus was reminding mature adults that they carry within them a childlike longing. Immaturity is the childish bent toward controlling our own destiny and securing gratification through controlling one's own fortune. The lilies of the field and the birds of the air, Jesus reminds us, do not attempt to control their lives but simply live their destiny as given by their Creator. When we come into alignment with the Kingdom of God we move out of the terrible dilemma of facing misfortune by attempting to control our own fortune.

Jesus told a parable of a man whose land produced a larger crop than he had room to store. He decided to build larger barns to store his abundant crop and then sit back and say, "Soul, you have ample goods laid up for many years; relax, eat, drink, be merry." But in the parable God spoke to him saying, " You fool! This very night your life is being demanded of you. And the things you have prepared, whose will they be?" (Luke 12:16-21) The man was a good man, but his intentions were out of alignment with the Kingdom of God.

Almost immediately after receiving commendation from Jesus for answering the question correctly, "You are the Messiah, the Son of the living God," Peter took Jesus aside and 'rebuked' him for saying that he was going to Jerusalem where he would experience suffering and even death. Jesus responded, "Get behind me, Satan! For you are a stumbling block to me; for you are setting your mind not on divine things but on human things" (Mt 16:21-23). Peter self-destructed after Jesus was arrested and he was accused of being one of his followers. "I do not know the man," Peter replied. Realizing what he had done, he went out and wept bitterly (Mt 26:72, 75). Peter was not a bad person despite Jesus' rhetorical reference to Satan; his intentions were good but were out of alignment with the Kingdom of God. Even worse, even though he meant well he attempted to throw Jesus out of alignment with the will of the Father. And then there is Judas whose zeal for his own version of the Kingdom led him to betray Jesus with a kiss. Drowning in remorse, he acknowledged his wrongdoing but then went out and hung himself (Mt 27:3-5). He was not an evil person but his intentions were out of alignment with the Kingdom of God. Being out of alignment with regard to hope can lead to self-destruction.

It is not enough to hope. One's hope must be in alignment with God's kingdom not our own version of it. False hope is a siren song enticing faith to raise its sails when there is no wind, as many have learned to their sorrow. On many an occasion when facing the loss of what we value the most, we 'keep our hopes up' that some miraculous intervention will occur and grant us our heart's desire. When our hope is finally crushed by the unavoidable reality of life, the sails of our faith lie tattered and torn at our feet.

In *After the Fall*, a play by Arthur Miller, Quentin surveys his life with a sad and cynical eye. He has two divorces behind him, a failed relationship where he attempted to save a desperate woman from suicidal self destruction by the power of love, and in ruins of a Nazi death camp a reminder of the murderous possibilities in the heart of otherwise normal people, including his own. He has a relationship with a German woman named Holga, a survivor of the collapse of a civilization into the ruins of war. Close to giving up all hope, Quentin ponders the mystery of her hope.

"That woman hopes!" he cries out. "Or is that exactly why she hopes, because she knows? What burning cities taught her and the death of love taught me: that we are very dangerous! And that, that's why I wake each morning like a boy--even now, even now! To know, and even happily, that we met unblessed; not in some garden of wax fruit and painted trees, that lie of Eden, but after, after the Fall, after many, many deaths... No, it's not certainty. I don't feel that. But it does seem feasible ... not to be afraid."

Miller reminds us that the capacity to hope lies on this side of Eden, where perfection and innocence no longer exist. With the loss of idealism, true hope is born. When the hope chest, with its cherished dreams of perfect love, is just another item at the yard sale, new hope arises as the reach of the human spirit for that which is at least feasible, if no longer fantastic.

Hope springs eternal in the human heart, so says the sage. All things considered, that is certainly true. But not everyone survives the loss of innocence when it comes to hope. The rebirth of hope out of the ashes of failure, like the mythical *phoenix*, is glorious in its appearance. But for some the ashes remain cold and dark. We admire hope as a virtue in those who survive the death of hope and yet continue to hope. As we bring hope into alignment with God as the only source of hope, we will learn what the apostle meant when he said of Abraham: "Hoping against hope, he believed that he would become 'the father of many nations,' according to what was said" (Rom 4:18). 'Hoping against hope' is the reach of the human spirit for the promises of God as inspired by the Spirit of God.

There is something about hope that defies explanation, much like the human spirit itself. We all know people whose spirit refuses to give up, who are moved by some invisible force that gives them a vision of a future which gives meaning and purpose for the present.

In Chapter Seven I quoted from a letter sent to me from prison by Linda Lee Smith, one of my students, who has served 28 years because she was in the house when her live-in boyfriend killed her two year-old daughter while her older daughter was also in the home. When the governor recently revoked the unanimous recommendation of the parole board (the eighth year in a row!) she wrote to me saying how difficult it was for her friends and even embarrassing for them when her parole was denied. But then she quickly realigned her hope and wrote to me: "I've finally found the concept that clarified this for me. I have too often confused the

OBJECT of my hope (the parole) with the SUBJECT of my hope—Christ Jesus. Instead of hoping 'for,' I must hope 'in.' I will not always get what I hope for, but I will never be disappointed by hoping in Christ." Linda is good at the repair work of hope.

Susie taught me a lesson that I shall never forget. Afflicted with cerebral palsy since birth, she cannot dress or feed herself. She talks with difficulty and in words which emerge as twisted and tortured as the spastic motions required to force them out. With a passion for life that exceeds most others less restrained by birth boundaries of their own, she completed college and a master's degree in theology, including several courses sitting in my classes.

When she received her degree, I once asked her what she intended to do, perceiving her within the boundaries which I had set for her. "Perhaps you will have a significant ministry to others who suffer handicaps in life," I suggested. "No," she said, "most of them haven't forgiven God for who they are, and I have."

Forgiving God for who I am! Indeed! Who should she hold responsible for the constricting birth boundaries which imprisoned her free and joyous spirit within a body she could not control? She expanded the horizon of her complaint, like Job of old, and laid the offense at the throne of God. When the Lord who created her did not dodge or duck, she concluded that the only freeing thing left was to forgive. Having lodged the charge against God with all of the emotional power at her disposal, she discovered that she also had the power to forgive him.

Susie did not suppose that God had caused her birth deformity nor did she feel that he had willed this condition for some inscrutable purpose of his own. Her dealings with God were not theological but deeply existential. She sought to touch with her feelings the face of God and trace out there the profile of one who would take responsibility for her life without looking away. In holding God responsible she found an ally in her predicament. Releasing God from blame became possible when God assumed responsibility. Her life now had two sides to it. The one side of her life was restricting and confining. The other side was open and freeing. This is what she meant by forgiving God for who she was. She let God become the other side to her life. This is the kind of repair work that keeps her aligned with the Kingdom of God.

When we live by the rhythm of the seasons we are kept from plunging directly from the long summer days into the winter's long night. There is important work to be done when the work of summer is done and before the work of spring begins. Putting everything back into working order is the important work of hope when there is no work to be done. Once we get our life back into working order, we can catch a new vision of what hope holds in store for us. "When the Lord restored the fortunes of Zion, we were like those who dream" cried the Psalmist (Ps 126:1). Dare to dream hope!

Chapter 14 - Visualizing

Expanding the Horizon of Hope

For now the winter is past, the rain is over and gone. The flowers appear on the earth; the time of singing has come, and the voice of the turtle-dove is heard in our land. The fig tree puts forth its figs, and the vines are in blossom; they give forth fragrance. Song of Solomon 2:11-13

Conventional wisdom tells us that young people are extravagant and often idealistic when it comes to hope but that with maturity hope is scaled down to a more realistic vision. In one sense that may be true, but when we look at what drives hope we see it in a different way. For example, when we are young it is typical to hope for what can get, often toys or even beyond that, material possessions, fame or freedom to go and do what we want. While hope expressed in this way is not always fantastic it is seldom realistic. We soon learn that we are not likely to receive everything we hope for and so, it is true, as we grow older we become more realistic about what life is going to give us.

At a certain point in the development of hope, we move from what we hope to get to what we hope to become. Even children soon learn to visualize themselves as becoming a person viewed by others as heroic or larger than life. Later this is turned more toward a vocational vision involving a career or profession. Again, we discover that the road to an illustrious career is a difficult one. We began to downsize our dreams, often out of financial necessity, physical limitations, lack of skill, or other responsibilities that creep into our lives and we begin to settle for something more realistic. So far, conventional wisdom has a convincing case. With maturity, youthful and idealistic hope tends to dream less and pick a spot to land on the near horizon.

It would be mistake however, to conclude from this that hope becomes near-sighted with age and more fatalistic as it becomes more realistic. This is not the kind of hope that comes with spiritual maturity. The spiritual gift of hope patiently waits for us to grow out of hoping for what we can get and what we can become in order to grow into the kind of hope that expands our horizon and enables us to visualize what we cannot see. The spiritual gift of hope empowers us when we let go of the immature and childish hope for what can get or become in life, to visualize what is given in life by embracing God's promise that often lies beyond the horizon.

This is the kind of hope that Abraham and Sarah embraced which transformed their vision and inspired their pilgrimage. "Hoping against hope," Abraham believed that Sarah would conceive though her womb was barren and even though his own body "was already as good as dead" (Rom 4:18-19). The author of the book of Hebrews describes this kind of hope as a pilgrimage; Abraham and Sarah were "looking forward to a city with eternal foundations, a city designed and built by God." All of these heroes of faith, "died still believing what God had promised them. They did not receive what was promised but they saw it all from a distance and welcomed it" (Heb 11:10, 13 NLT). This is not the kind of hope of which children dream; their visions are still within the horizon of what can be seen. To hope for that which is real but unseen is the kind of hope that gives assurance to faith (Heb 11:1).

When we look back at Abraham we see the progression of hope. In Paul's account Abraham received what he hoped for and became what he hoped to become. He gained a son that he desperately wanted and became the 'father of a multitude' (Rom 4). While Paul's purpose was to depict the righteousness of Abraham that he gained solely through faith, the hope that anchored that faith had not yet matured. It is only when we read the account provided by the author of the book of Hebrews that we discover how the horizon of his hope had expanded beyond what was visible and attainable as a present reality. "He looked forward to the city that has foundations" (Heb 11:10). Was the writer simply inspired to say that? Or did he look back and read the account through the lens of hope? One clue may be found in the message of the Angel of the Lord who spoke to Abraham after he had offered his son Isaac as a sacrifice to the Lord, the very child that he had hoped for. Abraham took the hope that he had produced through Sarah and gave it back to the Lord and in so doing expanded the horizon of his hope beyond what he could see, touch and hold. When the Lord intervened and Abraham received Isaac back again, from the dead as it were (Heb 11:19), the Angel of the Lord gave him a vision of a future where his offspring would be as numerous as the stars in heaven and the sand on the seashore (Gen 22:17). When Abraham obeyed God and offered up his 'hope-child' he not only received him back, but progressed to a more mature hope that could only be visualized as coming out of the future through the promise of God. This is the creative power of visualization. It expands the horizon of hope and revitalizes what is already as 'good as dead.'

The Creative Power of Visualization

During the long winter months on the farm in South Dakota where I grew up, a favorite pastime for my parents was reading the brightly colored seed catalogues that came in the mail. As they did this, they visualized the fruit, flowers and vegetables that they planned to grow the following summer. As I recall, the catalogues had no pictures of the seeds themselves, but of the blooming flowers and luscious fruit! While the metaphor of sowing seeds is a powerful one, it is the visualization of the harvest that stirs the imagination and inspires hope.

The planting of seed in the dark and damp soil in early spring is an exercise in hope, inspired by the vision of the fruit and the flower that will be produced by the warm sunny days of summer. The creative power of visualization that engenders hope as a future and invisible promise is captured by the human spirit as a component of present reality. Hope is a creative and life-enhancing vision created by the creative power of the spirit.

We can only grasp the reality of the spirit through some kind of illusion, says Ernest Becker in his Pulitzer prize winning book, *The Denial of Death*. Life enhancing illusions, he wrote, are those which arouse faith and produce the character necessary to face adversity with courage and conviction. Such illusions do not lie, but produce authentic faith in the spiritual realities which are true and eternal. There are illusions that lie. In other words, what we create out of our own imagination is often wishful thinking or unrealistic hopes that we invent in order to avoid dealing with present reality. By an illusion which does not lie, Becker means a symbol, picture, ritual or word which promises and points to a reality which is cherished and valued by the self but which cannot be directly grasped. A vow or promise between two people which intends to convey trust and love may be spoken or symbolized in a ritual. While the words can be heard and the symbol observed, the reality to which each points is invisible, but intended to be present and/or promised.

When Abraham and Sarah concocted a scheme to bring about God's promise through the servant maid, Hagar, they produced Ishmael and thought of him as the promised son, but it was an illusion that vanished when viewed in the light of God's creative Word. That a child could be conceived and born from a woman beyond the age of child-bearing and

whose womb was barren was an illusion that expanded the horizon of
hope for both Abraham and Sarah. That Isaac actual came into existence
is evidence of an illusion that did not lie.

Creative visualization is quite different from simply 'day-dreaming' or
projecting our own fantasy life on the screen of our imagination. Creative
visualization is similar to an illusion because there is 'more than meets
the eye.' We have become so familiar with the words of institution that
precede the offering of the elements of the Lord's Supper that we scarcely
notice that the reality of this event is a creative illusion where faith visual-
izes what cannot actually be seen (or tasted!). "This is my body broken
for you. This is my blood shed for you." But to take real bread and real
wine (or juice) as a participation in the life, death and resurrection of
Jesus expands the horizon of that event in such a way that it becomes a
'communion with the saints.'

In her marvelous little book, *Holy the Firm*, Pulitzer Prize-winning
author Annie Dillard, tells of being asked to buy communion wine for
the little church in which she worships on northern Puget Sound. "How
can I buy the communion wine? Who am I to buy communion wine? . .
. Shouldn't I be wearing robes and, especially a mask? Shouldn't I *make*
the communion wine? Are there holy grapes, is there holy ground, is
anything here holy? There are no holy grapes, there is no holy ground,
nor is there anyone here but us. . . There must be a rule for the purchase
of communion wine. 'Will that be cash, or charge?' . . . And so I'm out on
the road again walking, my right hand forgetting my left. I'm on the road
again walking, and toting a backload of God. Here is a bottle of wine with
a label, Christ with a cork. I bear holiness splintered into a vessel, very
God of very God, the sempiternal silence personal and brooding, bright
on the back of my ribs."

This is more than poetic imagery. She has the very words and promise
of Jesus that caused her to visualize a reality whose horizon lies beyond
the mere physical elements of bread and wine. Is that not also true with
regard to Jesus himself? The early creeds of the church sought to capture
the content of what they confessed when they called Jesus both true God
and also a true human being. Paul said that in Jesus "the whole fullness
of deity dwells bodily" (Col 2:11). Having said that how does one explain
that? We are here reminded of the saying of the Scottish Philosopher
Michael Polanyi whom I cited in Chapter Four, "We always know more
than we can tell." In other words, what cannot be comprehended can
be apprehended. We cannot always define exactly a reality that we can
visualize. In this case, visualization is a way of knowing something that

cannot be put into words.

Speaking of his own experience in the third person, the Apostle Paul wrote, "I know a person in Christ who fourteen years ago was caught up to the third heaven—whether in the body or out of the body I do not know; God knows. And I know that such a person—whether in the body or out of the body I do not know; God knows—was caught up into Paradise and heard things that are not to be told, that no mortal is permitted to repeat" (2 Cor 12:2-4). In an earlier letter Paul spoke of the kind of reality that is unknown to those who do not have the Spirit of God. "Those who are spiritual discern all things, and they are themselves subject to no one else's scrutiny" (1 Cor 2:15). In other words, don't ask me to prove by the mind what can only be visualized as a reality of the spirit.

Visualization is part of the grammar of hope. The book of revelation was no doubt originally written to give hope to those suffering persecution, and thus was 'coded' in the form of a series of visualizations that conveyed spiritual truth without causing suspicion to political enemies. John opens with an account in which he was "in the Spirit on the Lord's day," and had a vision of the Lord who revealed mysteries hidden from earthly eyes. He was then instructed to "write what you have seen" (Rev 1:10; 19). The writing as we all know, was almost entirely expressed in the form of visualization and was meant to be read as such. What might appear as strange even ridiculous illusions to those who do not possess the same spiritual gift of visualization as the author, are intended to be 'illusions that do not lie.' "These words are trustworthy and true," wrote John as he summed up his account (Rev 22:6). What faith believes must first be hoped for and as such, becomes the "assurance about things we cannot see" (Heb 11:1 NLT).

The use of visualization is common in the Bible. When God inspired Moses to lead the people out of Egypt the goal was only to be reached by a treacherous and monotonous journey through a waterless and inhospitable desert. After 400 years of existence as a slave people, the children of Israel were not a visionary people. What lay on the other side of this barren desert was beyond their horizon. The fact is, despite the description of the land of promise as 'flowing with milk and honey,' what we know as Palestine in those days was largely barren and infertile except for land close to the sea and the river. Even more recently a former Prime Minster of the state of Israel was heard to say concerning Moses, he might have been a great liberator of our people, but he led them to the only place in that region without oil! In calling Moses to lead the people out of Egypt instead of giving a more realistic description of the place to which they were to go, the Lord used visionary language; you will find there, he said, a land "flowing with milk and honey" (Exod 3:8). Those very words were repeated fourteen times in Leviticus, Numbers and Deuteronomy, and once again by Joshua when he exhorted the people after forty years of wandering through the desert to be courageous and enter in to possess the land (Joshua 5:6).

The Psalmist envisions the blessing of the Lord in a picture of a shepherd who guides the sheep to a place where there are "green pastures and still waters" which restore the soul. "You prepare a table before me in the presence of my enemies." The reader is stimulated to imagine the scene and to anticipate the blessing of "dwelling in the house of the Lord my whole life long" (Psalm 23). Visualization seeks to expand our horizons to experience a reality that cannot be explained but only envisioned. Visualization is a work of hope when there is no other work to be done. It is in fact, part of the seasonal life of hope. When the horizon of life becomes narrow and mean, visualize. When we do not get what we hope for and do not become who we hoped we would be, the options might be visualize or paralyze.

The words attributed to President John F. Kennedy at his inaugural address, "Ask not what your country can do for you, but ask what you can do for your country," were actually written fifty years earlier by the Lebanese philosopher and poet, Kahlil Gibran. In an article dedicated to his people in the Middle East, Gibran wrote, "Are you a politician asking what your country can do for you or a zealous one asking what you can do for your country?" Near the end of his article, Gibran wrote, "The children of tomorrow are the ones called by life, and they follow it with steady steps and heads high, they are the dawn of new frontiers, no smoke will veil their eyes and no jingle of chains will drown out their voices. They are few in number but the difference is as between a grain of wheat and a stack of hay. They are like the summits which can see and hear each other—not like caves, which cannot hear or see. They are the seed dropped by the hand of God in the field, breaking through its pod and waving its sapling leaves before the face of the sun."

Nearly a hundred years have passed since Gibran wrote these words. The people of his own land have lost his vision and are suffering the consequences. The ancient prophet of Israel wrote, "Where there is no vision, the people perish" (Prov 29:18 KJV). A modern translation reads, "When people do not accept divine guidance, they run wild" (NLT). In the face of despair and disillusionment, can hope be visualized?

The Practical Power of Visualization

Near the end of his life, after moving from the farm due to ill health, my father told me, "I never made much money farming. It was only when I hired someone to sit on the tractor while I went to the local livestock auction barn that I began to see that I could buy some cattle at a bargain price, feed them some grain and sell them at a much higher price." He then went on to say, "I discovered that too late to make much difference."

Indeed, he died not long after that leaving no debts but only a few thousand dollars which my mother carefully guarded and divided among the three of us children when she died. It is with some degree of pleasure that I was able to use the three or four thousand dollars that I inherited from my father's vision and my mother's frugality as an investment in my own vision of going to Scotland to study for a doctoral degree after serving eleven years as a pastor. Those few 'talents,' to use the expression in one of Jesus' parables, has been multiplied a thousand-fold in the visualization that caused me to expand the horizon beyond the end of a row of corn in South Dakota, beyond the last row of chairs in a church auditorium, and even beyond thirty years of teaching in a theological Seminary to the very writing of this book. Yes, visualization works!

The Austrian Psychiatrist Victor Frankl, who was himself a survivor of Auschwitz, reported that those prisoners who visualized life beyond the concentration camp, had a higher rate of survival than those who did not. He urged his fellow prisoners to imagine what it would be like to be released, to feast on their favorite food, to walk in the garden, to smell the flowers, and to be embraced by their loved ones. Those who did had a higher rate of survival despite their meager diet and brutal conditions.

Alan was one of my former students. Suffering a spinal cord injury in a motorcycle accident that left him paraplegic, he saw his dream of becoming a professional athlete crash and burn. When suicidal thoughts crept in during the early weeks of his hospitalization, he battled them with a will to live even though he could not grasp either content or purpose. Even without a means of making a living, he chose life. Without the means of caring for himself, he accepted care from others as a way of life. Drifting in the twilight zone of an ambiance that excused him from having to lift as much as a finger (literally!), he felt the air begin to move his wings (figuratively) and his spirit began to rise.

Having a nodding acquaintance with God through an untested and untroubled childhood faith, he began to respond to the trauma of his paralysis, and directed some pointed questions to the invisible deity that lurked around the edges of his consciousness. "All right God," he said one day, "You created the world out of nothing, let's see what you can do with me!"

In recounting this, Alan said that for the first time in his life, he viewed God as someone he could talk to without having to be sure of using the right words. "After all," he said, "What more could God do to me? If he didn't like it he could just turn away and leave me alone. I was not in a position to cause him any trouble."

He received no audible answer, no disembodied voice came to him with the cosmic vibes of a Charlton Heston. Nothing. But a strange stirring in his own spirit took place. "I felt like part of me had wings, " he said, "and I was lifted by an invisible breath so that I could see my situation from a different perspective. I gained a vision for what I might do within the limitations of my physical disability, and found a new hope for my life."

His soul was moved, I believe, by the Spirit of God and he gained the spiritual power of hope. Early in his life he hoped to find fulfillment and satisfaction through the attainment of a boyhood dream. When he awoke, his life was a nightmare and that hope died. Subsequently, through the brokenness of his spiritual life, and in the agony of his prayers, he had a profound sense of touching the face of God. "I felt like part of me had wings," he said, "and I was lifted by an invisible breath so that I could see my situation from a different perspective." While his legs remain paralyzed, the wings of his spirit carry him farther than he ever dreamed possible.

"I gained a vision for what I might do within the limitations of my physical disability, and found a new hope for my life," Alan told me in describing the turning point in his life following the accident which left him disabled. The progress he made in rehabilitation in learning to complete small tasks and care for himself even though confined to a wheel chair seemed directly related to the spiritual power of hope which he felt. He continued to visualize himself as functioning in creative and fulfilling ways and was empowered by this hope.

Thomas Moore suggests that visualization through positive images has a therapeutic effect both psychologically and physically. "As the traditional medicine of many peoples demonstrates, disease can be treated with images. The patient, for her part, needs to see the images of her healing, just as any of us in distress might look for the stories and images wrapped in our complaints."

Christian psychotherapists often use guided imagery as a way of helping people who suffer from unhealed trauma due to earlier emotional or physical injury. In visualizing a return to the time and place where the injury or abuse took place with Jesus as a guide, the power of Jesus to heal, forgive and release one from the bondage of the traumatic event can often produce a dramatic effect. The key of course, is not merely to revisit the former place and time of injury, that is the usually pattern of self-inflicted pain and wounding. But to visualize in the most elaborate and specific way the person of Jesus there as an advocate who virtually makes an intervention, merging present with past in such a way that the memory and power of the past is transformed.

Time after time when providing pastoral counseling to persons experiencing defeat and despair in their marriages, vocations, and personal relationships, my attempts at creating hope was met with a common refrain, "I see no hope in that." Life experience has a way of shrinking our horizon and limiting our vision to the tunnel rather than to the light at the end of the tunnel. When we speak of some having 'tunnel vision' we know that this person's horizon in life is narrow and constricted.

Visualization as a work of hope does not wait for the light to emerge at the end of the tunnel. Rather, through visualization one steps out of the tunnel and looks outward toward the horizon and sees the tunnel as from outside. "Thank God I am not that pitiful and depressed person in that tunnel!" I once visualized looking down at my small life from as great a distance as I could image and thought, "This is what God sees!" I then visualized my life as though I were looking back at it from a point where God was taking me. In order to do this I had to tilt my horizon as seen from where I was firmly fixed in place on earth in order to have a viewpoint from a horizon not visible from where I was standing. I thought of what Gibran wrote concerning those who are the 'children of tomorrow.' "They are like the summits which can see and hear each other—not like caves, which cannot hear or see." To hope in God is to be a 'child of tomorrow.' "I am going to prepare a place for you," Jesus said. "When everything is ready, I will come and get you, so that you will always be with me where I am" (John 14:3 NLT).

In my last visit to the place where I was born, I stood before the grave marker of my grandparents who both immigrated from Norway, visualizing a new life on the open Dakota prairie. On it was inscribed these words in the Norwegian language
SOV SØDT OG HVIL HOS GUD DIG UD
NAAR HAN TROR BEDST, HAN
SENDER BUD
Freely translated, it reads: Sleep well, and rest with God. In his best

time he will send for you. I live with hope, I sleep with hope, and rest in hope. It is always the season of hope on Jesus' calendar.

Chapter 15 - Planning

Practicing Hope as a Lifelong Journey

With barren earth and branches bared to bone,
Then only can the heart begin to know
The seeds of hope asleep beneath the snow;
Then only can the chastened spirit tap
The hidden faith still pulsing in the sap.

Only with winter-patience can we bring
The deep-desired, long-awaited spring.
Anne Morrow Lindbergh

My friend coaches high school football. Before a big game some years ago I told him that I hoped that his team would win. "Hope doesn't win ball games," he said. "We practice hard and work on our game plan." Having listened to commentators discuss the play-by-play progress of games on television I was familiar with the concept but asked him to tell me more. "Do you actually have a plan for the entire game, " I asked? "How can you possibly anticipate all of the possibilities that can occur during a game? After all, you can't control how the other team will react to the plays you call. Don't you just do the best you can and hope for a good outcome?"

"There's that word hope again," he replied. "You hope it doesn't snow on game-day but that's all you can do because the weather is outside of your control. The student body hopes that we will win the game, but they have nothing to do with whether we win or lose. Home field advantage might give us an edge, but that's mostly psychological not tactical. I plan for my team to win the game, but it all begins with a series of successful first downs."

I asked him to show me his game plan, and sure enough, he had the first touchdown all plotted out with a series of running and passing plays, each coded with its own number to be communicated by the coach to the quarterback. "But what if the other team has their own defensive game plan and you have to make a change."

"We have anticipated that too," he said. "My quarterback is trained to call an audible signal at the line of scrimmage; it's all part of the game-plan." I was impressed. "But what if a player is injured, especially the quarterback?" "We have a deep bench," he replied, 'and a backup quarterback who knows all of the plays."

I was more impressed. "Amazing," I said, "you must have your life so well organized that you have your life-time goals all plotted out and a game plan to achieve them!" There was a long pause. "Actually, it doesn't work that way in life, only in football. I do the best I can with my rather meager salary, try to provide well for my family and just hope that it all works out in the end."

"Ah," I replied, "there's that word hope again! Only this time you have no game plan to back it up. Being a Christian, I suppose that you just hope that God will provide for you and get you safely to heaven." He got a bit edgy at that and replied with what was intended to be a conversation-stopper. "When it comes to life, you can't plan for hope."

That did end the conversation and I have long pondered his statement. Can one really plan for hope or is hope by its very nature more like the weather than a first down, something that is outside of our control. If I can visualize what I hope for why cannot I create and execute a plan to achieve it? Is hope such a spiritual and therefore nebulous thing that it eludes my grasp when I try to plot it on the same page as I calculate my net worth? Have I somehow violated the sacred quality of a hope that I trust God to guard by having a back-up plan to put in place when the quarterback goes down? Or, have I trivialized and neutered hope by using it as an excuse not to have a game plan when it comes to something far more important than a football game?

I ask these questions in order to give myself permission to talk about hope as something that I not only visualize but plan for as deliberately and thoughtfully as I once spent winter days plotting and planning for next year's harvest by marking off on the calendar the days before spring planting. If I do not have a plan to execute with regard to what I visualize as hope I am only daydreaming. If I have no idea of what direction to take in arriving at the place where Jesus has gone to prepare for me, I might as well lie down and wait for him to come and get me. I am not sure that he would like that! If I have no plan by which to baptize the miscellaneous into the meaningful and no sacramental act that binds duty to my destiny I will be like children, "tossed to and fro and blown about by every wind of doctrine, by people's trickery, by their craftiness in deceitful scheming" (Eph 4:14). That's not good either.

"Work hard to show the results of your salvation," exhorts Paul, "for God is working in you, giving you the desire and the power to do what pleases him" (Phil 2:12-13 NLT). Put into action God's saving work, if that does not involve a plan I do not know what it means. Planning is intentional, it is practical, it is not merely something prior to action, it is the initial act itself.

When my friend prepares his team for the next game and yes, they do hope to win, they work the plan into practice so that it works on game-day. The fact that he could not and did not approach his own life of faith in the same way reveals the fact that what he hoped for was more a matter of luck than pluck. In other words, his theology of hope was more mythical than practical.

Can you plan for hope? Let me show you the ways.

Planning for Hope

Before I make a case for planning for hope, there is one text of Scripture that could be viewed as a conversation stopper. It is found in the book of James, which in many ways can be considered to be one of the most practical and down to earth epistles in the New Testament. James says: "Look here, you who say, 'Today or tomorrow we are going to a certain town and will stay there a year. We will do business there and make a profit.' How do you know what your life will be like tomorrow? Your life is like the morning fog—it's here a little while, then it's gone. What you ought to say is, 'If the Lord wants us to, we will live and do this or that.' Otherwise you are boasting about your own plans, and all such boasting is evil." James 4:13-17 NLT

First, the key to this passage is found in the last sentence. It is not planning itself that James warns against, but 'boasting about your plans.' Arrogance is the problem not the plan. To think that one can control the future by one's own efforts and ensure one's fortune in life by one's own intentions is not only arrogant it is folly. Jesus had something to say about such arrogance when he told the parable of the rich farmer who devised a plan to ensure his future through his own fortune. "You fool! This very night your life is being demanded of you. And the things you have prepared, whose shall they be" (Luke 12:16-21)? James is on the same track when he warns against the presumptuous use of planning as a means of controlling the future. When plans are made in this way planning is not toward hope but toward certainty. My friend the coach hopes that his team will win the game and he plans to win, but he knows that nothing is certain. The last thing that this coach wants is to be reported having said that his plan was perfect and the outcome of the game was an absolute certainty. Nonetheless, his game plan is 'planning for hope.'

In his parables of the Kingdom Jesus often stressed planning as just as important as action. "Which of you," Jesus said, "intending to build a tower, does not first sit down and estimate the cost, to see whether he has enough to complete it?" Or, "What king going out to wage war against another king, will not sit down first and consider whether he is able with ten thousand to oppose the one who comes against him with twenty thousand?" (Luke 14:28-32) "Be dressed for action and have your lamps lit," said Jesus, using the parable of those waiting for the wedding party (Luke 12:35; Mt 25:1-13). Again, in the parable of the talents, Jesus reinforced the point that what one hopes to receive or achieve depends on having an investment plan, putting the talent to work, rather than putting it in a safe place (Mt 25:14-30).

Planning is a means of shaping the vision of hope, it is the way in which we become a strategic part of God's mission. When Paul concluded that his mission was accomplished in the region of Asia, he caught a vision of Spain as the next place for him to go and proclaim the gospel of Christ. "My ambition has always been to preach the Good News where the name of Christ has never been heard" (Rom 15:20 NLT). As a result he began to plan. First he would go to Jerusalem to make sure that the money raised for the poor was safely delivered there. Then he would travel to the church at Rome, where he hoped that they would undertake to help him with the mission to Spain (Rom 14:23-29). What we have as his epistle to the Romans is actually part of his hope to reach Spain and his plan to enlist the church at Rome in this plan. Without Paul's plan for Spain there would be no book of Romans in the New Testament.

Planning is a means of plotting a vision where once there was only a vacancy. When hope is still a vision life remains an empty page, waiting for some characters to emerge, some symbols to give direction. Planning for hope places it on the map, tells us where to look when we are confused, what direction to take when we are lost, how far we have yet to go before we lay our head down for the last time. We need to know this.

Planning for hope is the first step in investing in hope. And those who invest in hope have a right to claim a share in hope.

The Apostle Paul, in defending his right as an apostle to be supported by the churches he has planted argued, "whoever plows should plow in hope and whoever threshes should thresh in hope of a share in the crop" (1 Cor 9:10). I resonate with that. I once planned to plow the field, sow the seed, and reap the harvest in the 'dead of winter' so to speak. The long hours sitting on the tractor in the cool and windy spring was working the plan, in hope of the harvest.

Planning is more than a metaphor drawn from the secular sphere, it is the work of hope; indeed it is our life-work and investment in the hope that lies before us. "So I run with purpose in ever step," Paul says of his own activity, using the analogy of one running a race; "I am not just shadow boxing," using another analogy. "I discipline my body like an athlete, training it to do what it should. Otherwise, I fear that after preaching to others I myself might be disqualified" (1 Cor 9:26-27 NLT). Paul's hope in Christ is not some vague, mystical prize floating in heavenly space. Rather it is a goal directly tied to his life-work. He cannot arrogantly claim it in advance, but it is a 'game plan' that he works out in daily practice.

It is not enough just to hope, we must have a plan for hope and practice the plan.

The Practice of Hope

The apostle Paul used the metaphor of an athlete training for a race. If hope is the finish-line where we receive the gift of eternal life, then what is often called a spiritual discipline should be viewed as practice for the game, not the game itself. By a spiritual discipline I mean times set aside from daily life for prayer, meditation, Scripture reading and even fasting in some cases. I fear, however, that what is often urged upon Christians as a regimen of spiritual discipline can end up more like an exercise in body-building than training for a game. Body-builders compete with one another for a more perfect body and even receive a trophy if they win the competition. This is hardly the kind of award that the apostle Paul had in mind when he spoke of 'disciplining his body like an athlete.' Following the direction that the metaphor points us, training is practice for a game. A spiritual discipline then ought to be considered to be a form of training or practice for the game. But what is the game? Clearly, for Paul the game is life lived out to the very end with hope in view to both inspire and reward the effort.

When we 'plan a worship service,' is the worship experience itself the fulfillment of the planning or should it be preparation for the game of life? What is the hope that inspires the planning? Is it for a more inspiring, exhilarating and sensational event? In that case, is it more like an event for body-builders in an arena than a spirited practice for the real game outside? Perhaps I have pushed the analogy too far. For I realize that authentic worship of God is more than practicing for something else. Worship, if truly an event in which God is involved through the liturgies of confession, absolution, praise, preaching and singing, has its own place in the curriculum of Kingdom living. But what I am reaching for is the distinction between planning, practicing and performing so that living hope embraces, enhances and inspires every time and place of our lives, to the very end.

I remember reading about American prisoners during the Vietnam War who spent years in captivity without resources to read and stimulate their daily life. Because some were Christians and had no Bibles, they agreed that each would write down whatever Scripture verses they had once memorized and now could remember. These were compiled as a kind of 'Reader's Digest' version of the Bible that could be passed around and used for study and meditation. I thought, now there was where the practice of spiritual discipline during earlier days counted when it came to the game of life. Without realizing it, when they learned some of the Scripture texts as a discipline earlier in their lives they were really planning for hope.

As an eighteen-year old member of the armed forces in basic training during the second World War, I experienced my first Christmas away from the church and family. We were confined to the barracks on Christmas Eve. In our loneliness and melancholy, someone began to sing a Christmas Carol. Those of us who had sung them year after year in church joined in. What became apparent however, much to our dismay, is that most of us could remember only the first verse, and then only the first part of the first verse! While we had sung these songs as part of our experience of Christmas in the context of the church, we had not practiced very well for the real game that took place in a bleak army barracks rather than a bright and colorful sanctuary. Our hope died out with each faltering verse, and we ended up more forlorn and pathetic than when we began.

We had not planned well for hope and we were apparently not well coached. We were in fact, as the apostle Paul said, like children, 'tossed to and fro' (Eph 4:14).

One of my distinguished faculty professors in seminary suffered a stroke soon after retiring. He was placed in an assisted living facility where he spent his days in a wheel chair, unable to speak. His once marvelous, disciplined and articulate voice was silence by a brain whose connection between thought and voice was broken. My friend, one of his former students and then dean of the seminary told me that when he went to visit him as he regularly did they could not converse but they could sing together. Growing up in a Baptist church this man who could no longer put words together in a sentence could still sing with gusto every word in the gospel hymns he had learned as a young man. While this is a testimony to the marvel and mystery of how our brains work, it is more than that. It is a reminder that hope is something you train for, it is something you practice for, it is something that you plan for.

Each time that I attend church and join in the worship service that has been *planned for me*, I wonder if it has been planned for such an outcome to my life. Am I practicing these songs, learning the words, imprinting the melody on my brain, or just being a cheerleader for a game that is never played? I do need to be inspired, I need to learn new chords and new words for the old ones. But I still need to practice and discipline my hope to keep it from wandering from one moment of inspiration to another. A coach that introduces new plays at every practice will never field a team that has the sense and discipline to make a first down, not to mention a touch down.

I know WHO is my hope, and I can sing it even now: "My hope is built on nothing less/ Than Jesus' blood and righteousness; I dare not trust the sweetest frame/ But wholly lean on Jesus' name." What songs of hope will I sing when I can no longer speak? Who is my coach? Who has a game plan for me that has hope written large at the end? Well, Jesus, of course. I know that. I confess that. But I also need to plan for that. I need to practice for that. I need to know what to do, where to look, what to believe when my coach calls the play.

I want to practice hard and faithfully. I need to learn the plays so that I can sing them from the heart. I want a clear vision of what lies ahead and a kind memory of what lies behind. I want fellow players who will hand me over with gentle hands not hold me back with anxious hearts.

And when I come to the end, I want to be able to say, "Good, I have been hoping and planning for this all of my life."

Epilogue

Empowering Hope Through the Practice of Faith

"Faith is the confidence that what we hope for will actually happen; it
gives us assurance of things we cannot see." Heb 11:1 NLT

Faith and hope are symbiotic siblings. Not only do they have their
origin in the same promise of God (they are siblings), they are dependent
upon each other for their existence (they are symbiotic). While this book
has hope as its major theme, faith has played a supporting role. It is time
to give faith its due. Hope depends on faith in the same way that brain-
waves depend upon muscles to transform vision into action. Faith is
muscular while hope is visionary. Hope envisions a harvest, faith plants a
seed. Hope dreams while faith digs. Hope rises and falls with the seasons,
faith plots a course and sticks to it. Hope says, "it is promised to you,"
faith says, "I believe it."

The author of the book of Hebrews says that "Faith is the confidence
that what we hope for will actually happen" (Heb 11:1). I remember
viewing a television news report during the Katrina hurricane disaster
that struck New Orleans in 2006. A National Guard general was standing
in the midst of the chaos accompanied by a major under his command.
"Major," the general said, "I need a convoy established in this part of the
city to carry in supplies. Can you make it happen?" The major saluted
and replied, "Yes sir, I can make it happen." He did not say, "I will do
my best," or "I will try," he left no room for excuses and simply said, "I
can make it happen."

This is exactly what faith says to hope. Hope envisions a harvest, faith
says, "I can make it happen," and begins preparing the soil and planting
the seed. Without hope, faith is aimless and pointless. Hope inspires faith
and calls it into action. Without faith, hope dreams but never awakens;

and even if it should awaken nothing has been done.

Let me now speak of the kind of faith that becomes the confidence of hope.

Faith at work is apparently more pleasing to God than faith at rest. The profession of faith is fine, wrote James, but what good is it without works? "Even the demons believe," James reminded his readers. For James, faith that didn't work was of no practical value. While others made great claims to faith, James countered, "By my works I will show you my faith" (James 2:18-19). The kind of works to which James refers is not the 'works of the law' that Paul rejects as unacceptable to God. Nor is the kind of faith that only becomes an empty profession of the lips acceptable to God. This is very much the same as what James means when he uses the example of Abraham whose "faith and actions worked together" in order to make faith complete (James 2:22 NLT).

The 'way of faith' as Paul describes it has to do with belonging to Christ not merely professing a belief in Christ (Gal 3:10-13; 23). Belonging to Christ is active, not passive. "Our believing is conditioned at its source by our belonging," wrote Michael Polanyi. Belief is not merely an intellectual affirmation of what is true. One cannot say, "I believe that I belong to God," without first experiencing that belonging. Thus, the truth of being in a relation with God is not a 'faith statement' but rather a 'faith practice.' The only thing that counts, says Paul, "is faith working through love" (Gal 5:6). The Greek word used is *energeō*, that is, "faith *energized* through love." This is what I call the practice of faith. This is what empowers hope.

My most recent visit to the dentist turned out to be with the son of the man who had been my regular dentist. He had recently completed dental school and was now establishing his own practice. I commented with a smile, "So, now that you have finished your schooling you are now going to practice!" He took it in good humor, "Yes, we hear that a lot. I guess that practice is not a good word, but it is an honorable one in our profession. It's a life calling, it's where we do what we have been taught."

As I reflected on that statement, I thought, "That's it. That's what I am trying to say about hope and faith." The promise of hope can be taught; we learn the grammar of hope through the story of salvation history. God created human beings and put something of his own spirit within them as a longing for more than the inevitable mortality resulting from being created out of the dust of the ground. The garden where the first humans emerged was good but it was also dangerous. A slip and fall occurred that appeared to be fatal, but hope revived along with the promise of a future that required the practice of faith. Yes, God clothed their nakedness with the skin of an animal and a new relationship was established, but now sacrifice became a ritual of renewal (Gen 2-4).

The practice became something that could be manipulated, and what was meant as a means to an end became an end in itself. Ritual became religion and religion without hope became more of a burden than a blessing. Jesus of Nazareth was born of this tradition, "born of a woman, subject to the law. God sent him to buy freedom for us who were slaves to the law, so that he could adopt us as his very own children" (Gal 4:4-5 NLT). After his baptism and anointing by the Spirit, Jesus set up his own practice of faith as one 'born from above;' "I have come down from heaven," he said (John 6:38). "I am the living bread that came down from heaven. Whoever eats of this bread will live forever" (John 6:51).

This is what we learn about hope. Our hope is in Jesus Christ who lived, died and was raised from the dead so that we might receive the gift of eternal life as a present down payment on a future inheritance (Eph 1:14). Paul puts it plainly: "He has rescued us from the power of darkness and transferred us into the Kingdom of his beloved Son, in whom we have redemption, the forgiveness of our sins" (Col 1:13-14).

This I learned in the school of faith. This was the hope that was promised to me through faith. This is how the practice of faith came to empower that hope.

At an early age I came to the realization that when I saw infants being baptized in the small Lutheran church in South Dakota where I lived with my family, that this at one time happened to me. I had no memory of it, of course, but was told of the time that I too was presented for baptism and that this was the beginning of a relationship with God that was given to me as a gift of grace. It was explained that just as I was born into this family through no choice or merit of my own, I was born into God's family through the grace of God, adopted as Paul said (Gal 4:5). It was as simple as that. Every baptism I witnessed seemed to make my own baptism a fact rather than merely a story. In my early teen-age years I was then enrolled in a year-long confirmation class where I learned by memory the correct answers to the catechism questions and what the Creeds meant and why they were important to believe. As it turned out, the practice of faith only began some years later. With my confirmation service where I answered for myself and spoke for myself with regard to what had been promised on my behalf, I had finished the 'school of faith.' But now I was being sent forth to 'practice' my faith. Little did I realize at the time what that meant. Perhaps even those who led me through the process did not understand what the practice of faith really meant as a life-long calling. Or, it may be that one cannot really enter into the practice of faith without some higher level of maturity. Even Jesus did not begin the practice of his faith until he was almost thirty years old. Being filled with the Spirit at his baptism he was empowered for the practice of faith. He endured temptation, was obedient unto death and grasped the hope set before him in confidence that his Father would bring him back from the dead (Mt 16:21; Phil 2:7-8).

Those who demonstrate exceptional faith appear to have a vision that propels them into extraordinary action. Such faith is a central theme in the Bible. It is a quality attributed to Noah when told to build the ark. "I can make it happen," Noah said. It was by faith that Abraham was declared righteous and along with Sarah, received the promise through which their family and all the families of the earth would be blessed (Gen 12). Not only did Abraham leave his family and country to set out on a pilgrimage to a new land, he went out "not knowing where he was going" (Heb 11:8). When he arrived in the land that he understood to be his inheritance from God, he found that it was occupied by natives who were not about to move over and give title to him. No matter. "He looked to the city that has foundations" and lived as a nomad and pilgrim in the land promised to him. When he despaired of having a son, being "as good as dead," through faith he received a son from his barren wife when he was close to one hundred years old (11:12).

The faith of Abraham and Sarah was captured by a vision, passed on from one generation to another. They went out, as the author of Hebrews said, "not knowing where they were going!" Yet, the call was to go forward, not back. The vision of faith is supplied by hope.

We go to church to confess our faith in God. To be sure that the words are proper and not lacking in theological content, they are printed for us in the liturgy and sung in the creed. We cannot be trusted to be spontaneous at such a crucial moment. A confession of faith in the sanctuary, as some have discovered, is easier to make than the living out of faith in the secular world.

Saving faith is not what one needs to do in order to be saved, but it is the kind of actions required of one who already belongs through the grace of God. Hope precedes faith and summons faith into action. God's promise of the gift of eternal life comes as good news, it is gospel because it is grace. The gospel of grace comes as a vision of hope arousing faith into action. It is faith that empowers this hope by implanting it into the soil of our daily life, tending this seed of hope, pulling the noxious weeds of doubt and despair, attending to it as it approaches the harvest of righteousness. "Those who are peacemakers will plant seeds of peace and reap a harvest of righteousness (James 3:18 NLT). Paul adds, "for we will reap at harvest time, if we do not give up" (Gal 6:9).

The Danish theologian, Søren Kierkegaard, often viewed as the founder of Christian existentialism, fell in love with a young woman, Regina Olsen. It was, by his own admission, an "instant love affair" that lasted for several years until he ended it by his own decision, for her own good as he put it, even though he continued to love her. He could write about faith but he could not practice it. Later in life he wrote, "Had I had faith I would have remained with Regina." His hope for marriage was put to death by his own hands due to lack of faith.

In contrast with Kierkegaard, the Swedish diplomat Dag Hammarskjold (1905-1961), himself a brooding, lonely but visionary man of faith wrote what may have been intended as his own obituary. This is the kind of faith I would like to practice. Here faith and hope walk hand-in-hand.

"He broke fresh ground--because, and only because, he had the courage to go ahead without asking whether others were following or even understood. He had no need for the divided responsibility in which others seek to be safe from ridicule, because he had been granted a faith which required no confirmation--a contact with reality, light and intense like the touch of a loved hand; a union in self-surrender without self-destruction, where his heart was lucid and his mind loving."

References

Preface

The reference to Arthur Miller is from, *After the Fall*. Copyright, 1964, *Arthur Miller's Collected Plays*, Volume II (New York: Viking Press, 1981).

The quotation from Thomas Wolfe is from, *Look Homeward Angel!* (New York: Charles Scribner's Sons, 1930), from the Frontispiece. "Which of us has known his brother? Which of us has looked into his father's heart? Which of us had not remained forever prison-pent? Which of us is not forever a stranger and alone? . . . Remembering speechlessly we seek the great forgotten language, the lost-lane-end into heaven, a stone, a leaf, an unfound door. Where? When?"

I have included in the preface to each of the four parts, a poem I wrote for my grandchildren. By including these I sought to capture and convey some pulse that moves through each part. If that is not self-evident, then simply accept them as a literary act of self indulgence; it is my book and I can put in it whatever I wish!

Chapter One

The quotation from Edna St. Vincent Millay, is from "Wine From these Grapes," Sonnet #10, *Collected Poems*, edited by Norman Millay (New York: Harper and Row, ND), p. 710.

The reference to the 2,000 year-old seed is Matthew Kalman, San Francisco Chronicle, Chronicle Foreign Service, Sunday, June 12, 2005.

The quotation from Heidegger is from, Martin Heidegger, *Essays in Metaphysics* (New York: Philosophical Library, 1960), p. 59.

Chapter Two

The poem by Anne Morrow Lindberg is from, "Second Sowing," in *The Unicorn* (New York: Pantheon Books, 1956), p. 32.

The citation from Dietrich Bonhoeffer is from, *Love Letters from Cell 92: The Correspondence between Dietrich Bonhoeffer and Maria Von Wedemeyer 1943-45*, edited by Ruth-Alice von Bismarck and Ulrich Kabit, translated by John Brownjohn (Nashville: Abingdon Press, 1995), pp. 245-46.

The quotation from Gerald May is from: "Entering the Emptiness," in *Simpler Living, Compassionate Life*, ed. Michael Schur (Denver: Living the Good News, 1999), p. 48.

Chapter Three
The story of Edye Smith is from the *People Magazine*, April 20, 2000, pp. 58-9.

Chapter Four
The prayer from Oscar Romero is cited in *Action in Waiting*, by Christoph Blumhardt (Farmington, PA: The Plough Publishing House, 1998), pp. xxx-xxxi. Salvador. See also: http://salt.claretianpubs.org/romero/romero.html

The quotation from Thomas Wolfe is from, *Look Homeward Angel!* (New York: Charles Scribner's Sons), 1930, from the Frontispiece.

The reference to Michael Polanyi is from, *The Tacit Dimension* (New York: Doubleday and Company, 1966), p. 4.

The quotation from Donald M. MacKinnon is from, *Borderlands of Theology*, (London: Lutterworth Press, 1968), p. 214.

Chapter Six)
The quotation from James Houston is from, *Joyful Exiles: Life in Christ on the Dangerous Edge of Things* (InterVarsity, 2006), p. 135.

The quotation from Dietrich Bonhoeffer is from, *The Cost of Discipleship* (London: SCM, 1964), p. 146.

The quotation from Annie Dillard is from, *Holy the Firm* (New York: Harper and Row, 1977), p. 55.

The second quotation from Dietrich Bonhoeffer is found in, *Sanctorum Communio* (Communion of Saints), 1927, first published, 1930 (Fortress Press, 1998 edition), p. 198.

The quotation from John Macmurray is from, *Persons in Relation* (London: Faber and Faber, Ltd., 1961), pp. 150, 159.

Chapter Eight
The quotation from Frederick Nietzsche is from, Sämtliche Werke: Kritische Studienausgabe, vol. 2, p. 627, eds. Giorgio Colli and Mazzino Montinari, Berlin, de Gruyter (1980). The Wanderer and His Shadow, aphorism 176, "The Patient Ones," (1880).

The quotation from Dietrich Bonhoeffer: is from, *Meditating on the Word* (Cambridge, MA: Cowley Publications, 1986), p. 139.

The quotations on the ultimate and the penultimate from Dietrich Bonhoeffer are from, *Ethics* (New York: Simon and Schuster, 1995), pp. 125-126, 133.

The quotation from Elizabeth Barrett Browning is from, *Sonnets from the Portuguese* (Mt. Vernon, New York: Peter Pauper Press, ND), p. 54.

Chapter Nine
The quotation from Ben Quash is found in, "The Play Beyond the

Play," in *Sounding the Depths: Theology through the Arts*, ed. Jeremy Begbie (London: SCM, 2002), pp. 102-3.

Chapter Ten

The citation from Irenaeus is from: *Irenaeus Against Heresies*, Volume 1, p. 334 (III/17/1).

Chapter Eleven

The song, 'Bringing in the Sheaves,' is from: *Church Service Hymns* (Winona Lake, IL: The Rodeheaver Hall-Mack Co., 1948), p 401.

The quotations on the ultimate and the penultimate from Dietrich Bonhoeffer are from, *Ethics* (New York: Simon and Schuster, 1995), pp. 125-126.

The quotation from John Macmurray is from, *Persons in Relation* (London: Faber and Faber, Ltd., 1970), p. 65.

The text of the hymn, "We Give Thee But Thine Own," is by William How, *The Hymnal for Worship and Celebration* (Waco, TX: Word Music, 1986), p. 620.

Chapter Twelve

The citation from Wendy Farley, is from *Tragic Vision and Divine Compassion* (Louisville: Westminster John Knox Press, 1990), p. 125.

The poem by Ridgely Torrence is from, "The Son," *Miami Poets*, William Pratt, editor (Oxford, Ohio: Friends of the Library Society, Miami University, 1988), p. 62.

The quotation by Sumerset Maugham is from, *Of Human Bondage* (New York: Bantom Books, 1991), pp. 48-49.

The poem by Lisel Mueller is from her book, *Alive Together* (Baton Rouge: Louisiana State University Press, 1996).

Chapter Thirteen

The reference to Søren Kierkegaard is from, *Purity of Heart is to Will One Thing* (New York: Harper and Brothers, A Harper Torchbook, 1956).

The quotation by Arthur Miller is from, *After the Fall* (New York: The Viking Press, 1972), pp. 113-4.

Chapter Fourteen

The reference to Ernest Becker is from his book, *The Denial of Death* (New York: Macmillan, The Free Press, 1973), pp. 158; 199; 202; 204.

The reference to Vicktor Frankl is from his book, *From Death-camp to Existentialism: A Psychiatrist's Path to a New Therapy* (Boston: Beacon Press, 1959).

The quotation from Annie Dillard is from her book, *Holy the Firm* (New York: Harper and Row, 1977), pp. 63-64.

The quotation by Kahlil Gibran is from, *The Treasured Writings of Kahlil Gibran* (Edison, NJ: Castle Books, 1951), pp. 774-779.

The quotation from Thomas Moore is from: *Care of the Soul: A Guide for Cultivating Depth and Sacredness in Everyday Life* (New York: Harper Collins, 1992), pp. 169-170.

Chapter Fifteen

The quotation by Anne Morrow Lindberg is from "No Harvest Ripening: Autumn 1939, *The Unicorn: And Other Poems, 1935-1955* (New York: Pantheon, 1956), pp. 40-41.

Epilogue

The quotation by Michael Polanyi is from *Personal Knowledge* (London: Routledge and Kegan Paul, 1958), p. 322.

The reference to Søren Kierkegaard is from *The Journals of Søren Kierkegaard* (New York: Harper Torchbooks, 1958), p. 86.

The quotation from Dag Hammarskjold is from: *Markings* (New York: Knopf, 1966), p. 110.

Index

CPSIA information can be obtained
at www.ICGtesting.com
Printed in the USA
LVHW081610150920
666080LV00028B/1024

9 781556 358142